—"Excellent info on regaining scriptural thinking and taking thoughts captive!"
— very informative and useful."

FOR AS I THINK I AM IN MY HEART SO I AM

Combining Biblical Counseling with Cognitive Behavioral Therapy

EDWARD D. ANDREWS

Second Edition

FOR AS I THINK IN MY HEART SO I AM

Combining Biblical Counseling with Cognitive Behavioral Therapy

[Second Edition]

Edward D. Andrews

Christian Publishing House
Cambridge, Ohio

FOR AS I THINK IN MY HEART - SO I AM: Combining Biblical Counseling with Cognitive Behavioral Therapy by Edward D. Andrews

ISBN-10: 1945757221

ISBN-13: 978-1945757228

Table of Contents

Preface

In a world that increasingly seeks quick fixes to profound emotional and spiritual challenges, the integration of Biblical Counseling with Cognitive Behavioral Therapy (CBT) offers a unique and deeply transformative approach. This book, *For As I Think In My Heart - So I Am*, presents a method that combines the timeless wisdom of the Bible with the practical strategies of CBT, providing readers with the tools they need to address the root causes of their struggles and to cultivate a life that honors God.

The foundation of this work rests on the conviction that true healing and growth can only be achieved when our minds are renewed by the Word of God (Romans 12:2). While Cognitive Behavioral Therapy has been recognized for its effectiveness in addressing patterns of thought that contribute to emotional and psychological distress, it is the Word of God that offers the ultimate truth and guidance needed to overcome these challenges. This book is designed to guide readers through a process of self-examination, repentance, and transformation, grounded in the belief that we are all created in the image of God and that our thoughts and actions should reflect this divine truth.

Each chapter of this book addresses specific areas of life where individuals commonly struggle, from dealing with destructive thoughts and managing emotions, to overcoming temptation and cultivating self-control. The integration of Biblical Counseling with CBT is not merely about managing symptoms or modifying behavior, but about leading readers to a deeper understanding of themselves and their relationship with God. The goal is to help readers develop a biblically grounded mindset that equips them to face life's challenges with faith, wisdom, and resilience.

This second edition expands upon the original work by incorporating new insights and practical applications, ensuring that the content remains relevant and accessible to a contemporary audience. The inclusion of updated examples and additional scriptural references serves to deepen the reader's understanding and application of the material.

I invite you, the reader, to approach this book with an open heart and mind, ready to engage with the truths of Scripture and the practical strategies of Cognitive Behavioral Therapy. As you journey through these pages, may you find the guidance and encouragement you need to align your thoughts with God's truth, and in doing so, experience the transformative power of His Word in every area of your life.

Edward D. Andrews

Author of 220+ books

Introduction

In the complexities of modern life, many individuals find themselves wrestling with deep-seated emotional struggles, persistent negative thoughts, and patterns of behavior that seem impossible to break. These challenges often stem from a combination of spiritual, emotional, and cognitive factors that are deeply intertwined. While secular approaches to counseling and therapy may offer some relief, they often lack the spiritual depth necessary to bring about lasting transformation.

For As I Think In My Heart - So I Am is not just another self-help book; it is a call to a deeper, more meaningful change that touches every aspect of a person's life. The title itself, drawn from the scriptural principle found in Proverbs 23:7, emphasizes that our thoughts shape who we are and what we become. If we are to live lives that reflect the character of Christ, our minds must be renewed, and our hearts aligned with the truths of Scripture.

This book presents a comprehensive approach that integrates Biblical Counseling with Cognitive Behavioral Therapy (CBT), two powerful tools that, when combined, offer a holistic path to healing and growth. Biblical Counseling anchors this journey in the unchanging truths of God's Word, providing the spiritual foundation necessary for true transformation. Cognitive Behavioral Therapy, on the other hand, offers practical techniques for identifying and changing harmful thought patterns, empowering individuals to take control of their emotional and mental well-being.

The approach taken in this book is both practical and deeply spiritual. It acknowledges the reality of human frailty, the impact of sin, and the need for God's grace in every aspect of our lives. At the same time, it provides clear, actionable steps that readers can take to cultivate self-control, overcome destructive behaviors, and develop a mindset that is in harmony with God's will.

Throughout this book, you will find that prayer is not presented as a standalone solution but as part of a broader process of seeking God's guidance and then acting on that guidance with intentionality and discipline. True transformation requires more than just asking for help; it requires a willingness to partner with God in the process, to study His Word diligently, and to apply its principles in every area of life.

This book is designed for those who are serious about making lasting changes in their lives. Whether you are struggling with anxiety, anger, temptation, or any other issue addressed in these pages, you will find the guidance you need to not only understand the root of the problem but also to take practical steps toward overcoming it.

In a world where the mind is constantly bombarded with messages that often contradict the teachings of Scripture, many Christians find themselves struggling to reconcile their faith with their thoughts and emotions. The gap between what we believe and how we think can sometimes feel insurmountable, leading to a dissonance that affects every aspect of our lives—our relationships, our decisions, and even our spiritual growth.

This book, *For As I Think In My Heart - So I Am*, was born out of a deep desire to bridge that gap. It seeks to provide a roadmap for Christians who are wrestling with the complexities of their inner world, using a powerful combination of Biblical Counseling and Cognitive Behavioral Therapy (CBT). These two disciplines, while distinct in their origins and methods, intersect in a profound way that offers believers both spiritual guidance and practical tools for mental and emotional well-being.

The Bible teaches us that our thoughts have a direct impact on our lives: "For as he thinks in his heart, so is he" (Proverbs 23:7). Yet, many of us live with patterns of thinking that are not only unhelpful but also unbiblical—patterns that lead to anxiety, depression, and a host of other challenges. Cognitive Behavioral Therapy, a widely respected psychological approach, helps individuals identify and change these destructive thought patterns. However, when CBT is combined with the truths of Scripture, it becomes a tool not only for mental clarity but for spiritual transformation.

This book does not offer a superficial or temporary solution to life's difficulties. Instead, it invites you to embark on a journey of deep reflection and intentional change. Each chapter addresses a specific area of life, from managing destructive thoughts to cultivating self-control, and provides biblically grounded strategies that align with the principles of CBT. The aim is not merely to change behavior but to renew the mind (Romans 12:2) in a way that reflects the character of Christ.

As you read, you will be challenged to examine your thoughts and beliefs through the lens of Scripture. You will be encouraged to replace lies with truth, to develop habits that foster spiritual growth, and to rely on God's Word as the ultimate authority in your life. This process will not always be easy, but it is essential for those who desire to live in a way that honors God and reflects His love and wisdom.

The integration of Biblical Counseling with Cognitive Behavioral Therapy presented in this book is designed to be practical, accessible, and deeply rooted in Scripture. Whether you are a pastor, a counselor, or a believer seeking personal growth, this book is a resource that will equip you with the tools you need to navigate the complexities of the mind and the heart in a way that is both biblically faithful and practically effective.

Let this journey begin with a prayerful heart, a willingness to be transformed by the renewing of your mind, and a commitment to apply the truths of God's Word to every thought and action. In doing so, you will discover the peace and strength that come from aligning your mind with the mind of Christ.

CHAPTER 1 We are All Born into Slavery

The concept of being born into slavery is a profound and biblical truth that echoes throughout Scripture. It is a fundamental aspect of Christian doctrine that touches the core of human existence and our relationship with God. Understanding this concept is crucial for anyone seeking to combine Biblical Counseling with Cognitive Behavioral Therapy (CBT). The Bible offers a clear and unambiguous diagnosis of the human condition, and this understanding forms the foundation for addressing the deeper issues of the mind and heart.

The Nature of Human Sinfulness

The Bible unequivocally teaches that every human being is born into a state of sin. This is not merely a moral failing or a cultural condition but a fundamental aspect of our nature as fallen creatures. Genesis 6:5 captures this stark reality: "And Jehovah saw that the wickedness of man was great in the earth, and every intention of the thoughts of his heart was only evil continually." This verse reveals the depth of human depravity, emphasizing that our thoughts and intentions are inherently corrupt from birth. The extent of this corruption is further underscored in Genesis 8:21, where Jehovah states, "The intention of man's heart is evil from his youth."

This inherent sinfulness is not something that develops over time; it is present from the moment of birth. Jeremiah 17:9 describes the human heart as "deceitful above all things, and desperately sick; who can understand it?" The heart, in biblical terms, represents the center of our being—our thoughts, emotions, and will. The deceitfulness and sickness of the heart signify that every aspect of our humanity is tainted by sin. This is not a condition that we can remedy on our own, for the problem lies at the very core of our existence.

The Universal Nature of Sin

The apostle Paul in the New Testament further elucidates the universal nature of sin. Romans 5:12 declares, "Therefore, just as sin came into the world through one man, and death through sin, and so death spread to all men because all sinned." Here, Paul traces the origin of sin back to Adam, whose disobedience introduced sin into the world. This sin nature is inherited by all humanity, leading to spiritual death and separation from God. The phrase "because all sinned" indicates that sin is not merely an individual act but a pervasive condition that affects every human being.

Paul continues to describe the struggle with sin in Romans 7:21-25, where he writes, "So I find it to be a law that when I want to do right, evil lies close at hand. For I delight in the law of God, in my inner being, but I see in my members another law waging war against the law of my mind and making me captive to the law of sin that dwells in my members. Wretched man that I am! Who will deliver me from this body of death? Thanks be to God through Jesus Christ our Lord! So then, I myself serve the law of God with my mind, but with my flesh I serve the law of sin."

Paul's words reflect the inner conflict that every believer experiences—the desire to do good is constantly opposed by the presence of sin. This "law of sin" is not merely an external force but an internal reality that holds us captive. Even after coming to faith in Christ, believers continue to struggle with the remnants of their sinful nature. This ongoing battle is a reminder that we are still in need of God's grace and deliverance.

The Implications for Biblical Counseling and CBT

In the context of Biblical Counseling and CBT, the understanding that we are all born into slavery to sin has profound implications. Cognitive Behavioral Therapy is based on the premise that our thoughts influence our emotions and behaviors. While this is true, the Bible reveals that our thoughts are not neutral but are tainted by sin.

The "cognitive distortions" identified in CBT, such as all-or-nothing thinking, overgeneralization, and catastrophizing, are not merely irrational thought patterns; they are manifestations of our sinful nature.

The biblical counselor must recognize that these cognitive distortions are rooted in the deceitfulness of the heart. The goal of counseling, therefore, is not merely to correct faulty thinking but to address the underlying sin that gives rise to these thoughts. This requires a careful and compassionate application of biblical truth, helping individuals to see their need for God's grace and the transforming power of the Holy Spirit.

One of the key differences between secular CBT and a biblical approach is the recognition that true change comes not from within ourselves but from God. Jeremiah 17:9-10 continues, "I, Jehovah, search the heart and test the mind, to give every man according to his ways, according to the fruit of his deeds." God alone can search and test the heart, revealing the true nature of our thoughts and intentions. The biblical counselor, therefore, must rely on God's Word and the guidance of the Holy Spirit to expose and address the root of sinful thinking.

The Role of Scripture in Renewing the Mind

Romans 12:2 provides a crucial insight into the process of change: "Do not be conformed to this world, but be transformed by the renewal of your mind, that by testing you may discern what is the will of God, what is good and acceptable and perfect." The renewal of the mind is not a one-time event but an ongoing process of transformation. This transformation is accomplished through the application of Scripture, which reveals God's truth and exposes the lies that we have believed.

The biblical counselor's role is to help individuals apply the truth of Scripture to their specific struggles. This involves identifying the lies they have believed, replacing those lies with God's truth, and encouraging them to meditate on that truth until it becomes a part of their thinking. For example, someone struggling with feelings of worthlessness may need to meditate on passages like Psalm 139:13-14, which says, "For you formed my inward parts; you knitted me together in my mother's womb. I praise you, for I am fearfully and wonderfully made."

The process of renewing the mind also involves repentance, which is a change of mind that leads to a change of behavior. Acts 3:19 exhorts, "Repent therefore, and turn again, that your sins may be blotted out." Repentance is not merely feeling sorry for our sins but turning away from them and embracing God's truth. This is a critical aspect of biblical counseling, as it addresses not only the symptoms of sin but the root cause.

The Hope of Deliverance through Christ

While the Bible paints a grim picture of the human condition, it also offers the hope of deliverance through Jesus Christ. Romans 7:24-25 expresses this hope: "Wretched man that I am! Who will deliver me from this body of death? Thanks be to God through Jesus Christ our Lord!" Jesus is the only one who can deliver us from the slavery of sin. His death on the cross paid the penalty for our sins, and His resurrection offers the promise of new life.

In Biblical Counseling, this hope must be central. While CBT can offer temporary relief by addressing faulty thinking, true and lasting change comes only through the gospel of Jesus Christ. The counselor's task is to point individuals to Christ, helping them to understand the depth of their sin and the greatness of God's grace. This involves not only teaching them the truth of Scripture but also walking with them through the process of repentance and renewal.

The Power of the Holy Spirit in Transformation

Spiritual growth is facilitated by the Holy Spirit through the study and application of Scripture. Galatians 5:22-23 describes the fruit of the Spirit: "But the fruit of the Spirit is love, joy, peace, patience, kindness, goodness, faithfulness, gentleness, self-control; against such things there is no law." These qualities are developed in us as we immerse ourselves in God's Word and allow the Holy Spirit to work in our hearts. Just as praying for personal growth requires intentional effort, spiritual growth necessitates a commitment to studying and living out biblical truths.

In times of decision-making, the Holy Spirit provides wisdom and direction through the Scriptures. James 1:5 encourages us, "If any of you lacks wisdom, let him ask of God, who gives generously to all without reproach, and it will be given him." As we pray for wisdom, it is crucial to study God's Word to discern His will. Just as seeking employment involves actively applying for jobs, seeking God's guidance involves diligently searching the Scriptures and applying their principles to our decisions.

The Holy Spirit convicts us of sin and leads us toward transformation through God's Word. John 16:8 says, "And when he comes, he will convict the world concerning sin and righteousness and judgment." This conviction is a call to action, prompting us to align our lives with God's standards as revealed in Scripture. By studying and applying biblical teachings, we can respond to the Holy Spirit's conviction and experience genuine transformation in our lives.

The biblical counselor must also encourage those they are counseling to seek God's guidance through prayer and the study of His Word. This is not merely a therapeutic technique but a vital aspect of the Christian life. Psalm 119:105 declares, "Your word is a lamp to my feet and a light to my path." God's Word provides the direction and wisdom needed for navigating the challenges of life and overcoming the slavery of sin.

The Reality of Spiritual Warfare

Another critical aspect of understanding our slavery to sin is recognizing the reality of spiritual warfare. Ephesians 6:12 reminds us, "For we do not wrestle against flesh and blood, but against the rulers, against the authorities, against the cosmic powers over this present darkness, against the spiritual forces of evil in the heavenly places." Sin is not merely a human problem; it is part of a larger spiritual battle.

Satan and his forces seek to enslave individuals in sin, and this battle is fought in the mind and heart. The lies and temptations that lead to sinful thinking are often rooted in satanic deception. John 8:44 describes Satan as "a liar and the father of lies." Understanding the nature of this spiritual battle is crucial for effective counseling. The counselor must be equipped with the armor of God (Ephesians 6:13-17) and must help those they counsel to stand firm in the truth.

The Word of God is described as "the sword of the Spirit" (Ephesians 6:17), which is our primary weapon in this battle. Just as Jesus responded to Satan's temptations with Scripture (Matthew 4:1-11), so must we combat the lies and temptations that seek to enslave us. The counselor must teach and model the importance of Scripture in overcoming the power of sin and standing firm in the face of spiritual attacks.

The Necessity of Community and Accountability

While the battle against sin is deeply personal, it is not one that we are meant to fight alone. The Bible emphasizes the importance of community and accountability in the Christian life. Hebrews 10:24-25 exhorts, "And let us consider how to stir up one another to love and good works, not neglecting to meet together, as is the habit of some, but encouraging one another, and all the more as you see the Day drawing near."

In the context of counseling, this means that individuals should not only rely on the counselor but also seek support from the broader Christian community. The church is meant to be a place of mutual encouragement and accountability, where believers can bear one another's burdens (Galatians 6:2) and help each other grow in Christlikeness. The counselor should encourage those they counsel to engage in meaningful relationships within the church, where they can find support, encouragement, and accountability.

Accountability is particularly important when dealing with deeply ingrained patterns of sin. James 5:16 instructs, "Therefore, confess your sins to one another and pray for one another, that you may be healed." Confession and prayer are powerful tools in the battle against sin, and they should be a regular part of the counseling process. The counselor should create a safe and supportive environment where individuals feel comfortable confessing their struggles and seeking prayer.

The End Goal: Freedom in Christ

The ultimate goal of Biblical Counseling, as it is combined with Cognitive Behavioral Therapy, is not merely to alleviate symptoms or correct faulty thinking but to lead individuals to the freedom that is found in Christ. Galatians 5:1 declares, "For freedom Christ has set us free; stand firm therefore, and do not submit again to a yoke of slavery." This freedom is not just freedom from the consequences of sin but freedom from the power of sin.

In Christ, we are no longer slaves to sin but have been given new life and a new identity. Romans 6:6-7 affirms, "We know that our old self was crucified with him in order that the body of sin might be brought to nothing so that we would no longer be enslaved to sin. For one who has died has been set free from sin." This truth must be at the heart of the counseling process, as it provides the foundation for lasting change and transformation.

The biblical counselor must continually point individuals to the hope and freedom that is available in Christ. This involves helping them to understand their new identity in Christ, teaching them to live out that identity in daily life, and equipping them to resist the lies and temptations of the enemy. The transformation that comes through the gospel is not merely a change in behavior but a change in the very core of who we are.

The freedom that Christ offers is not just an abstract concept but a practical reality that can be experienced in every area of life. This freedom empowers individuals to live in a way that honors God and reflects His character. As individuals experience this freedom, they are able to overcome the patterns of sin that once enslaved them and to live in the fullness of life that God intends for them.

In conclusion, while we are all born into slavery to sin, the Bible offers a clear and powerful message of hope and deliverance through Jesus Christ. Biblical Counseling, when combined with Cognitive Behavioral Therapy, provides a framework for addressing the deep-seated issues of the mind and heart. By grounding the counseling process in the truth of Scripture and relying on the guidance of the Holy Spirit, individuals can experience true transformation and freedom in Christ.

CHAPTER 2 How Are We to Understand the Psychology of Men?

Understanding the psychology of men is an endeavor that necessitates a biblical perspective, as the Bible offers the most accurate and insightful understanding of human nature, particularly the nature of men. The secular field of psychology often approaches the subject with theories and assumptions that are rooted in humanistic philosophies. However, when we turn to Scripture, we find a comprehensive framework for understanding men as created beings who bear the image of God, yet who are also deeply affected by the fall into sin. In this chapter, we will explore the biblical foundations for understanding the psychology of men, integrating these insights with the practical applications of Cognitive Behavioral Therapy (CBT) to provide a holistic approach to counseling.

The Biblical Concept of Manhood

The Bible begins with a clear statement of the nature of man in Genesis 1:26-27: "Then God said, 'Let us make man in our image, after our likeness. And let them have dominion over the fish of the sea and over the birds of the heavens and over the livestock and over all the earth and over every creeping thing that creeps on the earth.' So God created man in his own image, in the image of God he created him; male and female he created them." This passage establishes that men, like women, are made in the image of God. This concept, known as the Imago Dei, is foundational to understanding the psychology of men.

Being made in the image of God means that men possess certain qualities that reflect God's nature, such as rationality, morality, creativity, and relationality. However, it also implies that men are inherently relational beings, created to be in fellowship with God and others. This relational aspect is crucial when considering the psychological makeup of men, as it underscores the importance of relationships in shaping a man's identity and mental health.

In Genesis 2:18, we read, "Then Jehovah God said, 'It is not good that the man should be alone; I will make him a helper fit for him.'" This statement reveals that men are not created to be isolated individuals but are designed for companionship and community. The need for relationship is intrinsic to male psychology, and any counseling approach that neglects this aspect will be incomplete.

The Impact of the Fall on Male Psychology

While men were created in the image of God and designed for relationship, the fall into sin has profoundly affected male psychology. Genesis 3 records the disobedience of Adam and Eve, resulting in the entrance of sin into the world. This event had devastating consequences for all of humanity, including a distortion of the male psyche.

Genesis 3:16-19 outlines the specific consequences of the fall for men: "To Adam he said, 'Because you have listened to the voice of your wife and have eaten of the tree of which I commanded you, "You shall not eat of it," cursed is the ground because of you; in pain you shall eat of it all the days of your life; thorns and thistles it shall bring forth for you; and you shall eat the plants of the field. By the sweat of your face you shall eat bread, till you return to the ground, for out of it you were taken; for you are dust, and to dust you shall return.'"

The curse pronounced upon Adam highlights several key areas of male psychology that are affected by the fall:

1. **Work and Provision:** Men are called to work and provide for themselves and their families, but this task is now fraught with difficulty and frustration. The ground is cursed, and men must toil "by the sweat of [their] face" to provide for their needs. This struggle with work can lead to feelings of inadequacy, frustration, and a sense of futility, which are common psychological issues among men.

2. **Identity and Worth:** The fall introduced a distortion in how men perceive their identity and worth. Before the fall, Adam's identity was rooted in his relationship with God and his role as steward of creation. After the fall, men often seek their identity and worth in their work, achievements, or status, leading to a constant striving for significance and approval.
3. **Relational Struggles:** The fall also affected men's relationships, introducing conflict and competition. Adam's relationship with Eve became strained, and the harmony that existed between them was disrupted. This relational discord is evident in many aspects of male psychology, including struggles with intimacy, communication, and emotional vulnerability.

These consequences of the fall have deeply influenced the way men think, feel, and behave. Understanding these biblical truths is essential for addressing the psychological challenges that men face.

The Influence of Culture on Male Psychology

In addition to the impact of the fall, culture plays a significant role in shaping male psychology. From a biblical perspective, culture is understood as a human construct that is influenced by both the Imago Dei and the effects of sin. Therefore, while culture can reflect aspects of God's design, it can also distort and mislead.

One of the primary ways culture influences male psychology is through its definitions of masculinity. Many cultures promote a view of masculinity that is rooted in strength, independence, and dominance. While these traits are not inherently wrong, they can become problematic when they are divorced from biblical truth. For example, the cultural emphasis on independence can lead men to isolate themselves, avoid vulnerability, and resist seeking help, even when it is needed.

Proverbs 18:1 warns against this tendency: "Whoever isolates himself seeks his own desire; he breaks out against all sound judgment." Isolation is contrary to the relational nature of men as created in the image of God, and it often leads to psychological distress. Men who adopt a hyper-independent mindset may struggle with loneliness, depression, and an inability to form deep, meaningful relationships.

Another cultural influence is the pressure to achieve and succeed. Men are often judged by their accomplishments, career success, and financial status. While the Bible affirms the value of hard work and diligence (Proverbs 22:29), it also warns against the dangers of placing one's identity in material success. Ecclesiastes 2:11 reflects the futility of this pursuit: "Then I considered all that my hands had done and the toil I had expended in doing it, and behold, all was vanity and a striving after wind, and there was nothing to be gained under the sun."

The cultural pressure to succeed can lead to a distorted self-worth, where a man's value is tied to his achievements rather than his identity in Christ. This can result in anxiety, burnout, and a sense of emptiness, even when outwardly successful.

The Role of Emotions in Male Psychology

Emotions play a crucial role in male psychology, yet many men struggle to understand and express their emotions in healthy ways. The Bible provides valuable insights into the role of emotions in the life of a man.

Psalm 32:3-4 illustrates the psychological impact of unexpressed or unresolved emotions: "For when I kept silent, my bones wasted away through my groaning all day long. For day and night your hand was heavy upon me; my strength was dried up as by the heat of summer." This passage highlights the physical and psychological toll that suppressed emotions can take on a man.

Men are often socialized to suppress their emotions, viewing them as a sign of weakness. However, the Bible does not support this view. Scripture is replete with examples of men who expressed their emotions openly and honestly. King David, a man after God's own heart (1 Samuel 13:14), frequently poured out his emotions before God, as seen in the Psalms. David's example teaches that expressing emotions is not a sign of weakness but a vital aspect of a healthy relationship with God.

Jesus Himself, the perfect man, displayed a full range of emotions. He wept at the death of Lazarus (John 11:35), showed compassion for the multitudes (Matthew 9:36), expressed anger at the money changers in the temple (Matthew 21:12-13), and felt sorrow in the Garden of Gethsemane (Matthew 26:38). Jesus' emotional life demonstrates that emotions are a natural and healthy part of being human, and they should be expressed in ways that align with God's will.

In the context of counseling, it is important to help men understand that their emotions are not inherently wrong or sinful. Rather, emotions are part of the way God has designed us, and they can serve as indicators of what is happening in our hearts. Ephesians 4:26-27 instructs, "Be angry and do not sin; do not let the sun go down on your anger, and give no opportunity to the devil." This verse acknowledges that emotions like anger are not inherently sinful, but they must be managed in a way that does not lead to sin.

A key aspect of CBT in counseling men is helping them identify and challenge the thoughts that lead to unhealthy emotional responses. For example, a man who struggles with anger might be harboring thoughts of injustice or perceived threats to his status or identity. By examining these thoughts in light of Scripture, the counselor can help the man develop a more biblical perspective, leading to healthier emotional responses.

The Importance of Leadership and Responsibility

The Bible places a significant emphasis on the role of men as leaders, both in the family and within the broader community. Ephesians 5:23 states, "For the husband is the head of the wife even as Christ is the head of the church, his body, and is himself its Savior." This leadership role is not about dominance or control, but about responsibility and sacrificial love, as Christ demonstrated through His relationship with the church.

Understanding this aspect of male psychology is crucial in counseling, as many men struggle with the pressures and expectations of leadership. Some men may feel overwhelmed by the responsibility, leading to passivity or avoidance. Others may overcompensate by exerting control or dominance, which can lead to relational difficulties.

1 Peter 3:7 provides guidance on how men are to exercise their leadership: "Likewise, husbands, live with your wives in an understanding way, showing honor to the woman as the weaker vessel, since they are heirs with you of the grace of life, so that your prayers may not be hindered." This verse highlights the importance of understanding and honoring one's wife, which requires emotional intelligence and a servant-hearted approach to leadership.

In the context of CBT, helping men understand their God-given roles and responsibilities can be a key factor in their psychological well-being. This involves challenging cultural stereotypes of masculinity that equate leadership with power and control and instead promoting a biblical view of leadership as service and sacrifice. By aligning their thoughts and behaviors with biblical principles, men can experience greater fulfillment and effectiveness in their leadership roles.

The Role of Spirituality in Male Psychology

Spirituality is a central aspect of male psychology, as men are created with an innate need for a relationship with God. Ecclesiastes 3:11 states, "He has made everything beautiful in its time. Also, he has put eternity into man's heart, yet so that he cannot find out what God has done from the beginning to the end." This verse suggests that men have a deep, inherent awareness of the divine, which drives them to seek meaning and purpose beyond the material world.

However, this spiritual longing can be misdirected, leading men to seek fulfillment in things other than God, such as wealth, power, or pleasure. Romans 1:21-23 describes this tendency: "For although they knew God, they did not honor him as God or give thanks to him, but they became futile in their thinking, and their foolish hearts were darkened. Claiming to be wise, they became fools, and exchanged the glory of the immortal God for images resembling mortal man and birds and animals and creeping things."

In counseling, it is essential to address the spiritual dimension of male psychology. This involves helping men recognize their need for God and encouraging them to pursue a relationship with Him. Matthew 6:33 provides clear direction: "But seek first the kingdom of God and his righteousness, and all these things will be added to you." When men prioritize their relationship with God, other areas of their life fall into proper perspective, leading to greater peace and fulfillment.

CBT can be integrated with biblical spirituality by helping men identify and challenge thoughts that are rooted in idolatry or misplaced priorities. For example, a man who is consumed with the pursuit of wealth may be encouraged to examine the underlying beliefs driving this pursuit and to replace them with biblical truths about God's provision and the true source of contentment (1 Timothy 6:6-10).

Addressing Sexuality and Temptation

Sexuality is a significant aspect of male psychology, and the Bible provides clear guidelines for understanding and managing this area of life. Sexuality is a gift from God, intended to be enjoyed within the boundaries of marriage (Genesis 2:24; Hebrews 13:4). However, because of the fall, sexual desire can become distorted, leading to temptation and sin.

Jesus addressed the issue of sexual temptation in Matthew 5:27-28: "You have heard that it was said, 'You shall not commit adultery.' But I say to you that everyone who looks at a woman with lustful intent has already committed adultery with her in his heart." This passage emphasizes that sexual sin is not just a matter of outward behavior but begins in the heart and mind.

In counseling men, it is important to address the thought patterns that lead to sexual temptation. James 1:14-15 explains the process: "But each person is tempted when he is lured and enticed by his own desire. Then desire when it has conceived gives birth to sin, and sin when it is fully grown brings forth death." By helping men recognize and challenge these desires at the cognitive level, counselors can assist them in breaking the cycle of temptation and sin.

1 Corinthians 10:13 offers hope and encouragement: "No temptation has overtaken you that is not common to man. God is faithful, and he will not let you be tempted beyond your ability, but with the temptation he will also provide the way of escape, that you may be able to endure it." This verse reminds men that they are not alone in their struggles and that God provides the strength and resources needed to overcome temptation.

The Value of Accountability and Discipleship

Finally, an essential aspect of male psychology is the need for accountability and discipleship. Proverbs 27:17 states, "Iron sharpens iron, and one man sharpens another." This proverb highlights the importance of relationships in spiritual growth and character development. Men need the support and accountability of other godly men to help them stay on track in their walk with God.

In the context of counseling, encouraging men to engage in discipleship relationships can be a powerful tool for growth and transformation. This involves not only being discipled by a more mature believer but also investing in the lives of others. Matthew 28:19-20, known as the Great Commission, calls all believers to "make disciples of all nations." For men, this can be a source of purpose and fulfillment, as they pour into the lives of others and grow in their own faith.

James 5:16 reinforces the value of accountability: "Therefore, confess your sins to one another and pray for one another, that you may be healed. The prayer of a righteous person has great power as it is working." Confession and prayer within a community of believers are vital for overcoming sin and experiencing healing.

Integrating Biblical Counseling and CBT

As we consider the psychology of men from a biblical perspective, it becomes clear that the integration of Biblical Counseling and Cognitive Behavioral Therapy offers a powerful approach to addressing the unique challenges that men face. By grounding CBT techniques in the truth of Scripture, counselors can help men identify and correct the distorted thinking patterns that arise from their fallen nature, cultural influences, and personal experiences.

Philippians 4:8 provides a helpful framework for this integration: "Finally, brothers, whatever is true, whatever is honorable, whatever is just, whatever is pure, whatever is lovely, whatever is commendable, if there is any excellence, if there is anything worthy of praise, think about these things." This verse encourages men to focus their minds on what is true and good, replacing lies and distortions with the truth of God's Word.

Ultimately, the goal of combining Biblical Counseling with CBT is not merely to improve mental health or behavior but to facilitate deeper spiritual transformation. Romans 12:2 captures this vision: "Do not be conformed to this world, but be transformed by the renewal of your mind, that by testing you may discern what is the will of God, what is good and acceptable and perfect." As men's minds are renewed by the truth of Scripture, they will be better equipped to live out their God-given roles and responsibilities, experience healthy relationships, and walk in the freedom that Christ offers.

CHAPTER 3 How Are We to Understand the Psychology of Women?

Understanding the psychology of women from a biblical perspective is essential for any effective counseling approach. The Bible provides profound insights into the nature of women, their unique psychological makeup, and how these insights can be integrated into counseling practices. By grounding our understanding in Scripture, we can appreciate the distinctive qualities of women and address the specific challenges they face in a fallen world. This chapter will explore the biblical foundations for understanding the psychology of women, examining the impact of creation, the fall, cultural influences, emotions, relationships, and spirituality.

The Creation of Women: The Imago Dei and Relational Design

The foundation of understanding the psychology of women begins in Genesis, where the Bible records the creation of humanity. In Genesis 1:27, it is written, "So God created man in his own image, in the image of God he created him; male and female he created them." This verse establishes that women, like men, are created in the image of God (Imago Dei). This means that women reflect God's nature in their rationality, creativity, moral capacity, and relationality. Understanding this truth is crucial for grasping the inherent dignity and value of women.

The creation narrative continues in Genesis 2:18-24, where we see the unique creation of the woman: "Then Jehovah God said, 'It is not good that the man should be alone; I will make him a helper fit for him.' ... So Jehovah God caused a deep sleep to fall upon the man, and while he slept took one of his ribs and closed up its place with flesh. And the rib that Jehovah God had taken from the man he made into a woman and brought her to the man. Then the man said, 'This at last is bone of my bones and flesh of my flesh; she shall be called Woman, because she was taken out of Man.'"

This passage highlights several key aspects of female psychology:

1. **Relational Design:** Women are inherently relational beings. The fact that the woman was created as a "helper fit for him" underscores her role in relational dynamics. The term "helper" (Hebrew: ezer) is not a term of inferiority but rather one of complementary partnership. Women are designed for relationships, and this relational orientation profoundly shapes their psychological makeup.
2. **Distinctiveness and Equality:** While women are distinct from men, they are also equal in value and dignity. The woman's creation from Adam's rib signifies her equal standing as a partner in the human relationship. This equality in the image of God challenges any cultural notions that diminish the worth of women and affirms their inherent value.
3. **Unity in Diversity:** The creation of woman from man highlights the unity and diversity in God's design. Men and women are designed to complement one another, and this complementarity extends to their psychological makeup. Understanding this unity in diversity is essential for appreciating the differences between men and women without devaluing either gender.

The Impact of the Fall on Female Psychology

The fall into sin had profound effects on both men and women, distorting their psychological makeup and introducing challenges that continue to affect us today. Genesis 3 records the disobedience of Adam and Eve and the subsequent curse that resulted from their sin. For the woman, the consequences of the fall are particularly significant for understanding her psychology.

Genesis 3:16 states, "To the woman he said, 'I will surely multiply your pain in childbearing; in pain you shall bring forth children. Your desire shall be for your husband, and he shall rule over you.'" This verse highlights two key areas of female psychology affected by the fall:

1. **Pain in Childbearing:** The increased pain in childbearing is not limited to physical pain but extends to the emotional and psychological aspects of motherhood. The experience of bearing and raising children is fraught with both joy and sorrow, fulfillment and anxiety. This tension is a direct result of the fall and affects women's psychological experience of motherhood.
2. **Relational Struggles:** The phrase "your desire shall be for your husband, and he shall rule over you" points to the relational struggles that women experience as a result of the fall. This desire is not merely a romantic longing but a struggle for control and influence within the marital relationship. The fall introduced a power struggle into the male-female relationship, leading to tension and conflict. Understanding this dynamic is crucial for addressing relational issues in counseling.

The effects of the fall extend beyond these specific areas and influence every aspect of female psychology. Women, like men, struggle with sin, shame, fear, and the brokenness that results from living in a fallen world. Romans 3:23 reminds us, "For all have sinned and fall short of the glory of God." This universal truth applies to both men and women and is foundational for understanding the psychological challenges women face.

Cultural Influences on Female Psychology

Cultural influences play a significant role in shaping the psychology of women. While the Bible provides timeless truths about human nature, culture can distort these truths and impose unrealistic or harmful expectations on women. Understanding these cultural influences is essential for providing effective counseling.

One of the most pervasive cultural influences is the pressure on women to conform to certain standards of beauty, success, and behavior. Proverbs 31:30 speaks to this pressure: "Charm is deceitful, and beauty is vain, but a woman who fears Jehovah is to be praised." This verse challenges the cultural obsession with outward appearance and highlights the importance of inner character. The pressure to meet cultural standards of beauty can lead to a range of psychological issues, including low self-esteem, body image disorders, and anxiety.

Another cultural influence is the shifting expectations of women's roles in society. Women today are often expected to excel in multiple roles, including career, motherhood, and community involvement. While the Bible affirms the value of women in various roles (Proverbs 31:10-31), it also warns against the dangers of overextending oneself. Matthew 11:28-30 offers comfort and guidance: "Come to me, all who labor and are heavy laden, and I will give you rest. Take my yoke upon you, and learn from me, for I am gentle and lowly in heart, and you will find rest for your souls. For my yoke is easy, and my burden is light." Understanding the balance between cultural expectations and biblical priorities is crucial for addressing the psychological pressures women face.

The Role of Emotions in Female Psychology

Emotions play a significant role in female psychology, and the Bible provides valuable insights into how women can understand and manage their emotions in a godly way. Women are often more emotionally expressive than men, which can be both a strength and a challenge.

The Psalms provide numerous examples of emotional expression, and they serve as a model for how women can bring their emotions before God. Psalm 42:11 captures the struggle of emotional turmoil: "Why are you cast down, O my soul, and why are you in turmoil within me? Hope in God; for I shall again praise him, my salvation and my God." This verse acknowledges the reality of emotional distress while pointing to the hope that is found in God.

The Bible also emphasizes the importance of self-control and managing emotions in a way that honors God. Proverbs 25:28 states, "A man without self-control is like a city broken into and left without walls." This principle applies to women as well, highlighting the importance of cultivating self-control in the face of emotional challenges. In counseling, helping women develop healthy ways of processing and expressing their emotions is crucial for their psychological well-being.

It is also important to recognize that emotions can be influenced by various factors, including physical health, hormonal changes, and life circumstances. Understanding these factors can help women gain perspective on their emotions and seek appropriate help when needed.

The Significance of Relationships in Female Psychology

Relationships are central to female psychology, as women are inherently relational beings created for connection with others. The Bible emphasizes the importance of relationships in the life of a woman, including relationships with family, friends, and the broader community.

Titus 2:3-5 provides a picture of the importance of relationships among women: "Older women likewise are to be reverent in behavior, not slanderers or slaves to much wine. They are to teach what is good, and so train the young women to love their husbands and children, to be self-controlled, pure, working at home, kind, and submissive to their own husbands, that the word of God may not be reviled." This passage highlights the importance of mentorship and the role of older women in guiding and supporting younger women.

The Bible also addresses the unique challenges women face in relationships, including the potential for conflict, misunderstandings, and emotional pain. Ephesians 4:31-32 offers guidance for managing relational challenges: "Let all bitterness and wrath and anger and clamor and slander be put away from you, along with all malice. Be kind to one another, tenderhearted, forgiving one another, as God in Christ forgave you." These verses emphasize the importance of forgiveness, kindness, and tenderheartedness in maintaining healthy relationships.

In counseling, it is essential to help women navigate the complexities of their relationships, whether in marriage, family, friendships, or the church community. This involves addressing issues such as communication, conflict resolution, and setting healthy boundaries.

The Role of Spirituality in Female Psychology

Spirituality is a vital aspect of female psychology, as women have an inherent need for a relationship with God. The Bible provides a rich foundation for understanding the spiritual dimension of women's lives and how it influences their psychological well-being.

Luke 10:38-42 offers a glimpse into the spiritual life of women through the story of Mary and Martha: "Now as they went on their way, Jesus entered a village. And a woman named Martha welcomed him into her house. And she had a sister called Mary, who sat at the Lord's feet and listened to his teaching. But Martha was distracted with much serving. And she went up to him and said, 'Lord, do you not care that my sister has left me to serve alone? Tell her then to help me.' But the Lord answered her, 'Martha, Martha, you are anxious and troubled about many things, but one thing is necessary. Mary has chosen the good portion, which will not be taken away from her.'"

This passage highlights the importance of prioritizing spiritual growth and spending time in God's presence. Mary chose the "good portion" by sitting at Jesus' feet and listening to His teaching, while Martha was "anxious and troubled" by her responsibilities. This story illustrates the tension many women feel between their responsibilities and their spiritual lives.

In counseling, it is important to encourage women to prioritize their relationship with God and to find balance in their lives. This may involve helping them establish regular spiritual practices such as prayer, Bible study, and worship, as well as addressing any barriers to their spiritual growth.

The Bible also speaks to the unique ways in which women can serve God and others. Proverbs 31:20-21 describes a godly woman who "opens her hand to the poor and reaches out her hands to the needy. She is not afraid of snow for her household, for all her household are clothed in scarlet." This passage emphasizes the value of compassionate service and the impact women can have on their families and communities.

Addressing Sexuality and Temptation

Sexuality is an important aspect of female psychology, and the Bible provides clear guidance on how women can navigate this area of life in a way that honors God. Sexuality is a gift from God, designed to be enjoyed within the boundaries of marriage (Hebrews 13:4). However, the fallen nature of humanity means that women, like men, face temptations and challenges in this area.

1 Corinthians 6:18-20 provides important instruction on sexual purity: "Flee from sexual immorality. Every other sin a person commits is outside the body, but the sexually immoral person sins against his own body. Or do you not know that your body is a temple of the Holy Spirit within you, whom you have from God? You are not your own, for you were bought with a price. So glorify God in your body." This passage emphasizes the importance of fleeing from sexual immorality and recognizing the body as a temple of the Holy Spirit.

In counseling, it is important to help women understand the biblical principles of sexual purity and to address any distorted beliefs or behaviors in this area. This may involve addressing issues such as sexual temptation, pornography, and the emotional and psychological effects of sexual sin. Providing a safe and supportive environment for women to discuss these issues is essential for their healing and growth.

The Importance of Identity in Christ

A central aspect of female psychology is the issue of identity. Women, like men, are often tempted to find their identity in external factors such as appearance, achievements, or relationships. However, the Bible teaches that a woman's true identity is found in Christ.

Galatians 3:26-28 affirms this truth: "For in Christ Jesus you are all sons of God, through faith. For as many of you as were baptized into Christ have put on Christ. There is neither Jew nor Greek, there is neither slave nor free, there is no male and female, for you are all one in Christ Jesus." This passage emphasizes that in Christ, all believers share a common identity as children of God, regardless of gender or social status.

Understanding and embracing this identity is crucial for women's psychological well-being. When women place their identity in Christ, they are freed from the pressure to conform to societal standards or to find their worth in external factors. Instead, they can rest in the assurance of God's love and acceptance, knowing that they are valued and cherished as His daughters.

In counseling, it is important to help women explore their identity in Christ and to address any false beliefs or insecurities that may be hindering their spiritual and psychological growth. This may involve challenging cultural messages that promote a distorted view of womanhood and helping women develop a biblical perspective on their identity and worth.

The Role of Community and Accountability

Community and accountability are essential aspects of female psychology, as women are designed for relationships and mutual support. The Bible emphasizes the importance of community in the life of a believer, and this is especially true for women.

Acts 2:42 describes the early Christian community: "And they devoted themselves to the apostles' teaching and the fellowship, to the breaking of bread and the prayers." This verse highlights the importance of fellowship and mutual support in the Christian life. Women need the support and encouragement of other believers, and this is especially true in the context of counseling.

In counseling, it is important to encourage women to engage in meaningful relationships within the church community. This may involve participating in small groups, Bible studies, or mentorship relationships. Accountability is also crucial for helping women stay on track in their walk with God and in addressing specific areas of struggle.

Hebrews 10:24-25 offers further encouragement: "And let us consider how to stir up one another to love and good works, not neglecting to meet together, as is the habit of some, but encouraging one another, and all the more as you see the Day drawing near." This passage underscores the importance of regular fellowship and mutual encouragement in the Christian life.

Integrating Biblical Counseling with an Understanding of Female Psychology

Understanding the psychology of women from a biblical perspective provides a solid foundation for effective counseling. By grounding our approach in Scripture, we can address the unique challenges women face and help them grow in their relationship with God.

The goal of counseling is not merely to address psychological symptoms but to facilitate deeper spiritual transformation. Romans 12:2 captures this vision: "Do not be conformed to this world, but be transformed by the renewal of your mind, that by testing you may discern what is the will of God, what is good and acceptable and perfect." As women's minds are renewed by the truth of Scripture, they will be better equipped to navigate the challenges of life and to fulfill their God-given roles and responsibilities.

CHAPTER 4 How Can You Gain Control Over Your Feelings by Managing Your Irrational Thoughts?

Emotions are powerful and can often feel overwhelming, but they don't have to control your actions or dictate your life. The key to gaining control over your feelings lies in addressing the irrational thoughts that fuel them. Irrational thoughts are those distorted beliefs and assumptions that lead to negative emotions such as anxiety, anger, depression, or worthlessness. By identifying, challenging, and replacing these irrational thoughts with biblical truth and practical strategies, you can gain control over your emotions and live a life that aligns with God's will.

Understanding the Impact of Irrational Thinking

To gain control over your emotions, it's essential to first understand how irrational thinking contributes to emotional distress. Irrational thoughts often arise from absolute statements, negative self-talk, and unrealistic expectations. These thoughts distort reality and lead to emotions that are disproportionate to the situation.

For example, consider the thought, "I always mess everything up." This is an absolute statement that leaves no room for the truth that, while you may make mistakes, you also have successes and achievements. Such a thought pattern leads to feelings of worthlessness and hopelessness because it doesn't reflect the reality of your entire experience.

Romans 12:2 reminds us, "Do not be conformed to this world, but be transformed by the renewal of your mind, that by testing you may discern what is the will of God, what is good and acceptable and perfect." Renewing your mind involves challenging these irrational thoughts and replacing them with more balanced, truthful ones.

Identifying Irrational Thoughts

The first step in gaining control over your emotions is to identify the irrational thoughts that trigger them. This requires self-awareness and honesty. Pay attention to the thoughts that run through your mind when you're feeling upset, anxious, or depressed. Write them down if it helps you to see them more clearly.

For instance, if you struggle with feelings of worthlessness, you might notice thoughts like, "I never do anything right," or "No one cares about me." These thoughts are irrational because they are extreme and do not reflect the reality of your life or God's view of you.

To identify these thoughts, ask yourself:

- Am I using absolute language like "always" or "never"?
- Am I assuming that things will never change?
- Am I focusing only on the negative aspects of a situation?

Once you've identified these thoughts, it's time to examine them critically.

Challenging Irrational Thoughts with Truth

After identifying the irrational thoughts, the next step is to challenge them. This involves questioning the validity of these thoughts and comparing them with what you know to be true—both from your life experiences and from Scripture.

Take the thought, "I never do anything right." This thought is irrational because it's an absolute statement that doesn't consider the full picture of your life. To challenge this thought, ask yourself:

- Is it true that I never do anything right, or am I focusing only on my mistakes?

- What are some examples of things I've done well?
- How does this thought align with what God says about me in Scripture?

Philippians 4:8 provides a helpful guide for evaluating your thoughts: "Finally, brothers, whatever is true, whatever is honorable, whatever is just, whatever is pure, whatever is lovely, whatever is commendable, if there is any excellence, if there is anything worthy of praise, think about these things." If your thoughts don't meet these criteria, they are likely irrational and need to be challenged.

A more balanced thought might be, "I sometimes make mistakes, but I've also had many successes, and I can learn and grow from my experiences." This thought acknowledges both your weaknesses and strengths, providing a more accurate and constructive perspective.

Replacing Irrational Thoughts with Biblical Truth

Once you've challenged your irrational thoughts, the next step is to replace them with thoughts that are grounded in biblical truth and reflect a more accurate view of yourself and your situation.

If you struggle with thoughts of worthlessness, meditate on passages like Psalm 139:13-14: "For you formed my inward parts; you knitted me together in my mother's womb. I praise you, for I am fearfully and wonderfully made." This Scripture affirms your inherent value as a creation of God, counteracting the lie that you are worthless.

However, simply meditating on a verse isn't enough. You need to internalize it and let it shape your thinking. When the thought "I'm worthless" arises, counter it with the truth from Psalm 139. Remind yourself that, although you may have flaws and make mistakes, your worth is not defined by your performance but by your identity as a child of God.

Moreover, practice reframing your thoughts with more rational, biblical statements. Instead of saying, "I'm a failure," say, "I failed in this instance, but failure is not my identity. I can learn from this and do better next time." This kind of self-talk helps to align your emotions with reality and God's perspective.

Developing Practical Strategies for Managing Emotions

In addition to changing your thinking, it's important to develop practical strategies for managing your emotions when they arise. Here are some steps you can take:

1. **Practice Self-Awareness:** Stay aware of your emotional triggers and the thoughts that precede them. By catching irrational thoughts early, you can prevent them from escalating into overwhelming emotions.
2. **Use Scripture as a Weapon:** When you recognize an irrational thought, counter it immediately with Scripture. Ephesians 6:17 describes the Word of God as the "sword of the Spirit," which you can use to fight against the lies that lead to emotional turmoil.
3. **Engage in Positive Self-Talk:** Replace negative, irrational thoughts with positive, truthful statements. For example, if you think, "I can't handle this," replace it with, "With God's help, I can handle this one step at a time." Philippians 4:13 reminds us, "I can do all things through him who strengthens me."
4. **Set Realistic Expectations:** Avoid setting yourself up for failure by having unrealistic expectations. Understand that everyone makes mistakes and that growth is a process. Ecclesiastes 7:20 acknowledges, "Surely there is not a righteous man on earth who does good and never sins."
5. **Seek Accountability:** Find a trusted friend, mentor, or counselor who can help you stay accountable in managing your thoughts and emotions. Proverbs 27:17 says, "Iron sharpens iron, and one man sharpens another." This support can be invaluable in your journey toward emotional health.
6. **Pray for Wisdom and Strength:** Regularly ask God for the wisdom to recognize irrational thoughts and the strength to

replace them with truth. James 1:5 encourages us to seek God's wisdom: "If any of you lacks wisdom, let him ask God, who gives generously to all without reproach, and it will be given him."

7. **Practice Gratitude:** Gratitude shifts your focus from what is wrong to what is right. Regularly thank God for His blessings and for the ways He is working in your life. 1 Thessalonians 5:18 instructs, "Give thanks in all circumstances; for this is the will of God in Christ Jesus for you."
8. **Take Action:** Sometimes, the best way to manage emotions is to take action. If you're feeling overwhelmed, break down tasks into smaller steps and tackle them one by one. Taking action helps to reduce feelings of helplessness and gives you a sense of control.

Applying These Principles in Everyday Life

Managing your thoughts and emotions is not a one-time event but a daily practice. It requires vigilance, intentionality, and reliance on God's Word. By applying the principles outlined in this chapter, you can gain greater control over your feelings and live in a way that honors God.

Consider a situation where you feel anxious about an upcoming event. Your mind may be filled with irrational thoughts like, "I'm going to mess up," or "Everyone will think I'm a failure." To apply these principles, start by identifying these thoughts and recognizing them as irrational. Challenge them by asking, "Is it true that I always mess up?" and "Does it really matter what others think of me, or is it more important what God thinks?" Replace these thoughts with biblical truth, such as, "God is with me, and He will help me do my best" (Isaiah 41:10).

Next, use positive self-talk to reinforce this truth: "I have prepared for this event, and with God's help, I can handle whatever comes my way." Engage in prayer, asking God for peace and confidence. Take practical steps to prepare for the event, breaking tasks into manageable pieces, and reminding yourself of God's faithfulness.

By consistently applying these strategies, you'll find that your emotions become more manageable, and your responses more aligned with God's will. Over time, you'll develop greater emotional resilience and a deeper trust in God's provision and guidance.

CHAPTER 5 How Can We Overcome Our Struggle Against Human Weakness?

Human weakness is a reality that every person must confront. Whether it manifests as physical limitations, emotional vulnerabilities, or spiritual shortcomings, the struggle against our inherent weaknesses is a central part of the human experience. The Bible offers both a diagnosis of our condition and a path to overcoming these weaknesses through the power of God's truth, wisdom, and strength. This chapter will delve into the nature of human weakness, how it affects us, and practical, biblical strategies for overcoming these struggles.

Understanding the Nature of Human Weakness

Human weakness encompasses all aspects of our being—physical, emotional, mental, and spiritual. It is a condition that stems from our fallen nature, as described in the account of Adam and Eve's disobedience in Genesis 3. Romans 5:12 provides a succinct summary: "Therefore, just as sin came into the world through one man, and death through sin, and so death spread to all men because all sinned." The introduction of sin into the world brought with it the frailty of the human condition.

This weakness is not limited to moral failings but includes the broader reality of human limitations. Physically, we are susceptible to sickness, aging, and ultimately death. Emotionally, we are prone to fear, anxiety, and despair. Mentally, we can be plagued by confusion, doubt, and irrational thinking. Spiritually, we are often inclined to sin, struggle with faith, and feel distant from God.

Paul captures the essence of this struggle in Romans 7:18-19: "For I know that nothing good dwells in me, that is, in my flesh. For I have the desire to do what is right, but not the ability to carry it out. For I do not do the good I want, but the evil I do not want is what I keep on doing." This inner conflict is something that every believer faces—the desire to live righteously, coupled with the reality of our ongoing struggle with sin and weakness.

Recognizing the Impact of Human Weakness on Our Lives

The impact of human weakness can be seen in various areas of life. It affects our relationships, our work, our mental and emotional health, and our spiritual growth. For instance, a person who struggles with anxiety may find it difficult to form healthy relationships, as their fears cause them to withdraw or react defensively. Similarly, someone who battles with physical illness might find it challenging to fulfill their responsibilities, leading to feelings of inadequacy or frustration.

The Bible does not shy away from acknowledging these weaknesses but instead offers a way to confront and overcome them. In 2 Corinthians 12:9-10, Paul shares a profound truth he learned through his own struggles: "But he said to me, 'My grace is sufficient for you, for my power is made perfect in weakness.' Therefore I will boast all the more gladly of my weaknesses, so that the power of Christ may rest upon me. For the sake of Christ, then, I am content with weaknesses, insults, hardships, persecutions, and calamities. For when I am weak, then I am strong."

This passage reveals a critical principle for overcoming human weakness: It is not about eliminating our weaknesses but rather about relying on God's strength to carry us through. God's grace is not merely a passive favor but an active, empowering force that enables us to endure and thrive despite our limitations.

Practical Strategies for Overcoming Human Weakness

While acknowledging our weaknesses is the first step, it is essential to develop practical strategies rooted in biblical principles to overcome these struggles. Here are some key approaches:

1. **Relying on God's Strength:** The Bible repeatedly emphasizes that our strength comes not from ourselves but from God. Philippians 4:13 declares, "I can do all things through him who strengthens me." This verse is not a license for overconfidence but a reminder that our ability to overcome weakness is grounded in our reliance on God. When faced with situations that expose our limitations, we must turn to God in prayer, asking for His strength and guidance.

Practical Application: Start your day with prayer, asking God for the strength to face the challenges ahead. Throughout the day, when you encounter moments of weakness—whether physical, emotional, or spiritual—pause and reaffirm your reliance on God. Remind yourself of verses like 2 Corinthians 12:9, and speak them aloud if necessary to reinforce your trust in His power.

2. **Renewing Your Mind with God's Word:** Our thoughts play a significant role in how we perceive and respond to our weaknesses. Romans 12:2 encourages us to "be transformed by the renewal of your mind." This renewal process involves replacing negative, self-defeating thoughts with the truth of God's Word. For example, when you feel overwhelmed by your weaknesses, meditate on Scriptures that remind you of God's promises and faithfulness.

Practical Application: Identify specific areas of weakness where you struggle with negative thoughts. Find Scripture passages that address these areas and commit them to memory. Whenever these negative thoughts arise, counter them with the truth of God's Word. For instance, if you struggle with feelings of inadequacy, recall 2 Corinthians 3:5, which states, "Not that we are sufficient in ourselves to claim anything as coming from us, but our sufficiency is from God."

3. **Practicing Self-Discipline:** Human weakness often manifests in a lack of self-control, whether in our actions, emotions, or thoughts. Galatians 5:22-23 lists self-control as one of the fruits of the Spirit, indicating that it is a quality we can cultivate through the Holy Spirit's work in our lives. Developing self-discipline involves making intentional choices that align with God's will, even when it is difficult.

Practical Application: Set specific, achievable goals for areas where you struggle with self-discipline. For example, if you tend to procrastinate, create a daily schedule with clear deadlines and stick to it. If you struggle with controlling your emotions, practice mindfulness and take deep breaths before reacting to stressful situations. Regularly pray for the Holy Spirit's help in exercising self-control.

4. **Seeking Support from the Christian Community:** The Bible emphasizes the importance of fellowship and mutual support among believers. Ecclesiastes 4:9-10 reminds us, "Two are better than one, because they have a good reward for their toil. For if they fall, one will lift up his fellow. But woe to him who is alone when he falls and has not another to lift him up!" We are not meant to struggle against our weaknesses alone; God has given us the body of Christ to support and encourage one another.

Practical Application: Surround yourself with a community of believers who can offer encouragement, accountability, and prayer support. If you are struggling with a particular weakness, consider joining a small group or finding a mentor who can walk alongside you. Be open and honest about your struggles, and allow others to speak truth and encouragement into your life.

5. **Embracing Humility and Dependence on God:** One of the dangers of human weakness is the temptation to pridefully deny or minimize it. However, Scripture teaches that humility is the key to experiencing God's grace. James 4:6 states, "But he gives more grace. Therefore it says, 'God opposes the proud but gives grace to the humble.'" Admitting our weaknesses and our need for God's help is not a sign of failure but of wisdom.

Practical Application: Practice humility by regularly confessing your weaknesses to God in prayer. Acknowledge your need for His guidance and strength in every area of your life. When you experience victories or successes, give credit to God rather than taking pride in your own abilities. Remember that your strength comes from Him, not from yourself.

6. **Focusing on God's Purpose:** Understanding that God can use our weaknesses for His purposes can provide a powerful motivation to persevere. In Romans 8:28, we are reminded, "And we know that for those who love God all things work together for good, for those who are called according to his purpose." Even our weaknesses can be part of God's plan to shape us, teach us, and bring glory to Him.

Practical Application: Reflect on how God might be using your weaknesses to grow your faith, build your character, or fulfill His purposes in your life. Instead of viewing your weaknesses as obstacles, see them as opportunities for God to demonstrate His power and grace. Journal your experiences and how God has worked through your weaknesses, using them as reminders of His faithfulness.

7. **Staying Persistent in Prayer:** Persistent prayer is a vital tool in the battle against human weakness. Jesus taught the importance of persistence in prayer through the parable of the persistent widow in Luke 18:1-8. In the same way, we must be diligent in bringing our weaknesses before God, trusting that He hears and will respond according to His will.

Practical Application: Develop a consistent prayer routine where you bring your struggles and weaknesses before God. Don't just pray once and then forget about it—continue to seek God's help daily. Keep a prayer journal where you can record your requests and how God answers them over time. This practice will strengthen your faith and remind you of God's ongoing involvement in your life.

Applying These Strategies to Specific Areas of Weakness

To make these strategies more concrete, let's apply them to some common areas of human weakness.

Overcoming Physical Weakness:

Physical weakness can be one of the most challenging struggles, whether due to illness, disability, or aging. Psalm 73:26 offers comfort: "My flesh and my heart may fail, but God is the strength of my heart and my portion forever." While physical limitations are real, they do not define your value or usefulness in God's kingdom.

Practical Steps:

- Accept your limitations and focus on what you can do rather than what you can't.
- Pray for God's strength and healing, but also for contentment and peace in your current condition.
- Engage in activities that are within your physical capabilities, and find ways to serve others that do not strain your physical resources.

Overcoming Emotional Weakness:

Emotional weakness, such as anxiety, depression, or fear, can be debilitating. Isaiah 41:10 provides assurance: "Fear not, for I am with you; be not dismayed, for I am your God; I will strengthen you, I will help you, I will uphold you with my righteous right hand." God's presence is a constant source of emotional strength.

Practical Steps:

- Practice mindfulness and grounding techniques to manage overwhelming emotions.
- Meditate on Scriptures that speak to God's peace and presence in your life.

- Seek counseling or support groups where you can share your struggles and receive encouragement.

Overcoming Mental Weakness:

Mental weakness might include confusion, doubt, or a lack of clarity in decision-making. James 1:5 reassures us, "If any of you lacks wisdom, let him ask God, who gives generously to all without reproach, and it will be given him." God offers wisdom and guidance to those who seek it.

Practical Steps:

- Take time to pray and seek God's wisdom before making decisions.
- Write down your thoughts and concerns to gain clarity and perspective.
- Surround yourself with wise counselors who can offer guidance and insight.

Overcoming Spiritual Weakness:

Spiritual weakness is perhaps the most significant struggle, as it affects our relationship with God and our ability to live according to His will. Hebrews 4:16 encourages us: "Let us then with confidence draw near to the throne of grace, that we may receive mercy and find grace to help in time of need." We are invited to approach God boldly, knowing that He is ready to help us in our spiritual struggles.

Practical Steps:

- Commit to regular Bible study and prayer to strengthen your spiritual foundation.
- Participate in corporate worship and fellowship to stay connected to the body of Christ.
- Confess any known sin and seek God's forgiveness, trusting in His promise of restoration.

Conclusion: Living in Victory Over Weakness

While human weakness is an inevitable part of life, it does not have to define us. By relying on God's strength, renewing our minds with His Word, practicing self-discipline, seeking support from others, embracing humility, focusing on God's purpose, and staying persistent in prayer, we can overcome our weaknesses and live in the victory that Christ has secured for us.

Through these practical strategies, we are not only able to manage our weaknesses but to grow stronger in our faith and more reliant on God's power. As we continue to seek Him, we will find that His grace is indeed sufficient, and in our weakness, His strength is made perfect.

CHAPTER 6 How Can You Overcome Destructive Self-Defeating Thoughts?

Destructive self-defeating thoughts are a pervasive issue that can severely impact a person's emotional, mental, and spiritual well-being. These thoughts, often rooted in lies, misconceptions, and negative experiences, can lead to feelings of worthlessness, hopelessness, and despair. Overcoming these thoughts is not just about changing one's mindset; it's about aligning one's thinking with the truth of Scripture and taking practical, actionable steps to replace destructive patterns with healthy, God-honoring thoughts.

Understanding the Nature and Source of Destructive Self-Defeating Thoughts

Destructive self-defeating thoughts are those negative, irrational, and often harsh judgments we make about ourselves. They stem from a variety of sources, including past experiences, unmet expectations, cultural pressures, and, most importantly, spiritual warfare. These thoughts can manifest in statements like, "I'm not good enough," "I'll never succeed," or "God doesn't care about me."

The Bible makes it clear that these types of thoughts are contrary to the truth of who we are in Christ. John 8:44 identifies Satan as "the father of lies," and it is often through these lies that destructive thoughts take root. Satan seeks to undermine our identity in Christ and distort our perception of God's love and truth.

Ephesians 6:12 reminds us that "we do not wrestle against flesh and blood, but against the rulers, against the authorities, against the cosmic powers over this present darkness, against the spiritual forces of evil in the heavenly places." This verse highlights that the battle against destructive thoughts is not merely psychological but spiritual.

To combat these thoughts, we must engage with spiritual tools, particularly the Word of God.

Twelve Common Self-Defeating Thoughts

1. **All-or-Nothing Thinking (Black-and-White Thinking):**
    - **Explanation:** This is the tendency to see things in extremes, with no middle ground. You may think in absolutes, like "always," "never," or "completely."
    - **Example:** "If I don't get an A on this test, I'm a total failure." A person may believe that anything less than perfection is unacceptable, leading to feelings of failure and inadequacy.
2. **Overgeneralization:**
    - **Explanation:** This involves making a broad, sweeping statement based on a single event or limited evidence. It often involves using words like "always" or "never."
    - **Example:** "I got rejected from one job, so I'll never find employment." After a single setback, the person assumes they will consistently fail in similar situations.
3. **Mental Filtering:**
    - **Explanation:** Focusing solely on the negative aspects of a situation while ignoring the positives. This creates a distorted view of reality.
    - **Example:** "Everyone praised my presentation, but I stumbled on one word, so it was a disaster." The person disregards the positive feedback and fixates on the minor mistake.
4. **Disqualifying the Positive:**
    - **Explanation:** Automatically dismissing or invalidating positive experiences or achievements, often downplaying them as luck or unimportant.

- **Example:** "They only complimented my work because they felt sorry for me." The person denies the validity of positive reinforcement.

5. **Jumping to Conclusions:**
   - **Explanation:** Making negative assumptions without sufficient evidence. This includes mind-reading (assuming you know what others think) and fortune-telling (predicting negative outcomes).
   - **Example:** "I just know they don't like me," or "This project will definitely fail." The person presumes a negative outcome without concrete proof.

6. **Catastrophizing (Magnification):**
   - **Explanation:** Exaggerating the significance of a problem or situation, often imagining the worst possible outcome.
   - **Example:** "If I make one mistake at work, I'll get fired, and then I'll lose everything." The person inflates the potential consequences of a minor issue.

7. **Emotional Reasoning:**
   - **Explanation:** Believing that because you feel a certain way, it must be true, even if there's no evidence to support it.
   - **Example:** "I feel anxious, so there must be something wrong." The person assumes their feelings reflect reality.

8. **Should Statements:**
   - **Explanation:** Rigid, self-imposed rules about how you or others "should" act, often leading to feelings of guilt, frustration, or disappointment.
   - **Example:** "I should always be able to handle everything on my own," or "People should always be

kind." The person creates unrealistic expectations for themselves or others.

9. **Labeling and Mislabeling:**
    - o **Explanation:** Assigning a fixed, negative label to yourself or others based on a single behavior or event.
    - o **Example:** "I made a mistake, so I'm an idiot," or "She didn't answer my call, so she's a terrible friend." The person reduces their identity or others' identity to a negative trait or action.

10. **Personalization:**

- **Explanation:** Taking responsibility for events outside of your control or blaming yourself for things that aren't your fault.
- **Example:** "It's my fault the team didn't win," or "My child is struggling in school because I'm a bad parent." The person unjustly assumes responsibility for outcomes beyond their influence.

11. **Mind-Reading:**

- **Explanation:** Assuming you know what others are thinking about you, often leading to unnecessary anxiety or resentment.
- **Example:** "They didn't smile at me, so they must think I'm annoying." The person presumes negative judgments from others without any confirmation.

12. **Discounting Your Achievements:**

- **Explanation:** Downplaying or minimizing your successes by attributing them to luck or external factors rather than your efforts or abilities.
- **Example:** "I only got that promotion because no one else applied." The person fails to recognize their hard work and merit in achieving their goals.

These self-defeating thoughts create a cycle of negative thinking that can significantly impact one's emotional and spiritual well-being.

Recognizing these patterns is the first step toward replacing them with healthier, more constructive thoughts aligned with biblical truth.

Recognizing and Identifying Destructive Thoughts

The first step in overcoming self-defeating thoughts is recognizing and identifying them. Often, these thoughts become so ingrained that they operate almost unconsciously, influencing our emotions and behaviors without us even realizing it. To effectively address these thoughts, we must bring them into the light of consciousness.

Practical Steps:

- **Journaling:** Begin by keeping a thought journal. Write down any negative or self-defeating thoughts that come to mind throughout the day. Don't censor yourself—record the thoughts as they are. This practice will help you become more aware of the patterns and triggers of these thoughts.
- **Self-Reflection:** Take time each day to reflect on your thought patterns. Ask yourself, "What am I telling myself right now? Is this thought aligned with God's truth, or is it rooted in fear, insecurity, or lies?"
- **Prayer for Discernment:** Pray for the Holy Spirit's guidance to discern the source of your thoughts. James 1:5 encourages us, "If any of you lacks wisdom, let him ask God, who gives generously to all without reproach, and it will be given him." Ask God to reveal any lies you've believed and to give you clarity in recognizing them.

Challenging and Replacing Destructive Thoughts with Biblical Truth

Once you have identified the destructive thoughts, the next step is to challenge and replace them with the truth of God's Word. This process is at the heart of renewing the mind, as described in Romans

12:2, "Do not be conformed to this world, but be transformed by the renewal of your mind, that by testing you may discern what is the will of God, what is good and acceptable and perfect."

Practical Steps:

- **Evaluate the Evidence:** For each destructive thought, ask yourself, "Is this thought true? What evidence do I have to support or refute it?" Compare the thought with what Scripture says about you and your circumstances. For instance, if you think, "I'm a failure," counter this with the truth of Philippians 4:13, "I can do all things through him who strengthens me."
- **Scripture Meditation:** Identify specific Scriptures that directly counter your destructive thoughts. Meditate on these verses daily, allowing God's truth to saturate your mind and reshape your thinking. For example, if you struggle with thoughts of worthlessness, meditate on Psalm 139:14, "I praise you, for I am fearfully and wonderfully made."
- **Confession and Declaration:** Speak the truth out loud. There is power in confessing God's Word over your life. When a destructive thought arises, verbally reject it and declare the truth instead. For example, if the thought "God doesn't care about me" arises, say aloud, "God loves me, and He has promised never to leave me or forsake me" (Hebrews 13:5).

Developing a New Pattern of Thought: Practical Strategies

Overcoming destructive self-defeating thoughts is not a one-time event but an ongoing process that requires persistence and intentionality. Developing new, healthier patterns of thought involves both spiritual disciplines and practical actions.

Practical Steps:

- **Practice Gratitude:** Gratitude is a powerful antidote to negative thinking. 1 Thessalonians 5:18 instructs us to "give thanks in all circumstances; for this is the will of God in Christ Jesus for you." Each day, write down three things you are thankful for. This practice helps shift your focus from what's wrong to what's right, fostering a more positive and God-centered perspective.
- **Renewing Your Mind Through Prayer and Action:** As you pray for God's help in overcoming destructive thoughts, also commit to taking actionable steps. For instance, if you struggle with the thought, "I can't do anything right," commit to completing a task that you've been avoiding, no matter how small, and do it to the best of your ability. Then, thank God for the strength to accomplish it.
- **Set Achievable Goals:** Break down overwhelming tasks into smaller, manageable steps. This not only helps to combat feelings of inadequacy but also builds confidence as you achieve each step. Proverbs 16:3 encourages us, "Commit your work to Jehovah, and your plans will be established."
- **Surround Yourself with Encouragement:** Proverbs 27:17 says, "Iron sharpens iron, and one man sharpens another." Surround yourself with people who will speak truth and encouragement into your life. Whether it's a friend, a mentor, or a small group, having a support system is crucial in maintaining a healthy thought life.

Implementing Daily Practices to Maintain Victory Over Destructive Thoughts

Victory over destructive thoughts is maintained through daily, consistent practices that reinforce the truth of God's Word in your life. These practices help to solidify new, healthy thought patterns and prevent the reemergence of destructive thinking.

Practical Steps:

- **Daily Scripture Reading and Meditation:** Start each day by reading and meditating on Scripture. Choose verses that address your specific struggles and allow them to guide your thoughts throughout the day. Psalm 1:2-3 describes the blessed person whose "delight is in the law of Jehovah, and on his law he meditates day and night. He is like a tree planted by streams of water that yields its fruit in its season, and its leaf does not wither. In all that he does, he prospers."
- **Accountability Check-ins:** Regularly check in with an accountability partner who can help you stay on track with your thought life. Share your progress, your struggles, and your victories. Pray together and encourage one another to stay focused on God's truth.
- **Mindful Reflection:** At the end of each day, take time to reflect on your thoughts and emotions. Ask yourself, "Did I allow any destructive thoughts to take root today? How did I respond? What truth did I rely on?" This reflection helps you to stay aware of your thought patterns and make necessary adjustments.

Acting on Behalf of Your Prayers

Prayer is a vital part of overcoming destructive thoughts, but it must be paired with action. James 2:17 reminds us that "faith by itself, if it does not have works, is dead." It's not enough to pray for deliverance from negative thoughts; you must also take practical steps to renew your mind and align your thinking with God's truth.

Practical Steps:

- **Active Participation in Your Renewal:** When you pray for God to help you overcome destructive thoughts, be prepared to actively participate in that process. This might mean seeking counseling, attending a support group, or engaging in regular

Bible study. It also means being diligent in applying the truths you learn from Scripture to your daily life.

- **Create a Prayer and Action Plan:** After you pray, write down specific actions you will take to work on behalf of your prayers. For instance, if you pray for more patience with yourself, your action plan might include practicing self-compassion and avoiding negative self-talk. Philippians 4:6-7 encourages us to bring our requests to God in prayer, followed by the promise of His peace that "surpasses all understanding" when we actively trust Him.
- **Prayer Walks and Reflection:** Engage in prayer walks where you reflect on God's truth and ask for His strength to replace destructive thoughts. As you walk, consider the beauty of God's creation and His sovereignty over your life. Use this time to speak affirmations and Scriptures that counteract negative thinking.

Persevering Through Setbacks

It's important to acknowledge that overcoming destructive thoughts is a journey that may include setbacks. You might find yourself slipping back into old patterns of thinking, but it's crucial to persevere and continue applying the strategies you've learned.

Practical Steps:

- **Don't Be Discouraged by Setbacks:** Remember that setbacks are a normal part of the growth process. Instead of condemning yourself, return to God's grace and reaffirm your commitment to overcoming these thoughts. Lamentations 3:22-23 reassures us, "The steadfast love of Jehovah never ceases; his mercies never come to an end; they are new every morning; great is your faithfulness."
- **Return to Your Prayer and Action Plan:** When you experience a setback, revisit your prayer and action plan. Reflect on what triggered the setback and adjust your plan if

necessary. Seek God's guidance in prayer and ask for the strength to continue moving forward.

- **Reinforce Positive Changes:** Celebrate the progress you've made, no matter how small. Reinforcing positive changes helps to build momentum and encourages further growth. Reflect on Philippians 1:6, which reminds us that "he who began a good work in you will bring it to completion at the day of Jesus Christ."

Living in Freedom from Destructive Thoughts

The goal of overcoming destructive self-defeating thoughts is to live in the freedom that Christ offers. Galatians 5:1 declares, "For freedom Christ has set us free; stand firm therefore, and do not submit again to a yoke of slavery." By renewing your mind with God's truth, engaging in daily practices, and acting on behalf of your prayers, you can break free from the chains of destructive thinking and experience the abundant life that Jesus promises.

As you continue this journey, remember that you are not alone. God is with you, empowering you to overcome every thought that seeks to defeat you. Through His strength, you can renew your mind, transform your life, and walk in the victory that is yours in Christ.

CHAPTER 7 How Can You Diagnose Your Moods as the First Step Toward Healing?

Understanding and diagnosing your moods is the crucial first step in overcoming emotional challenges and moving toward a state of mental and spiritual well-being. Moods, those pervasive feelings that color your perception of reality, can significantly influence your thoughts, actions, and relationships. However, these emotional states often go unchecked, leading to patterns of behavior that may be destructive or misaligned with God's will. To effectively manage and improve your emotional health, it is essential to diagnose your moods with clarity, recognizing their triggers, and understanding their impact on your life. This chapter explores the process of diagnosing your moods, the spiritual significance of doing so, and practical strategies for moving forward in faith and healing.

The Importance of Recognizing Your Moods

Before you can address and manage your moods, you must first recognize them for what they are. Moods are often mistaken for fleeting emotions, but they tend to last longer and can influence your overall outlook on life. Unlike immediate emotional reactions, moods can linger for hours, days, or even longer, subtly shaping your thoughts and decisions.

The Bible speaks to the importance of self-awareness in understanding one's internal state. In Proverbs 4:23, we are advised to "keep your heart with all vigilance, for from it flow the springs of life." The heart in this context refers not only to the seat of emotions but also to the mind and will. Vigilance in guarding and understanding your heart includes being aware of your moods, as they are an integral part of your emotional and spiritual life.

When you fail to recognize your moods, you may find yourself acting out in ways that are inconsistent with your values or beliefs. For example, a persistent mood of irritability might lead you to snap at loved ones, even when there is no justifiable cause. Over time, unrecognized and unchecked moods can erode your relationships, your sense of self, and your relationship with God.

Diagnosing Your Moods: The Process of Self-Examination

Diagnosing your moods involves a process of self-examination, where you intentionally reflect on your emotional state and the factors contributing to it. This process is not just about labeling your moods but understanding their roots and their effects on your life.

Self-examination is a practice encouraged in Scripture. In Psalm 139:23-24, David prays, "Search me, O God, and know my heart! Try me and know my thoughts! And see if there be any grievous way in me, and lead me in the way everlasting!" This prayer reflects a desire for God to reveal the deeper aspects of one's heart and mind, including the moods that may be influencing thoughts and actions.

To diagnose your moods effectively, consider the following aspects:

1. **Identify the Mood:** Start by giving your mood a name. Are you feeling anxious, sad, angry, or apathetic? Putting a label on your mood helps to bring it into clearer focus.
2. **Recognize the Triggers:** Reflect on what may have triggered this mood. Was it a particular event, a conversation, or perhaps even a lack of something—like rest or time with God? Identifying triggers is crucial because it helps you understand what circumstances or thoughts are leading to your current state.
3. **Assess the Duration:** Consider how long you have been in this mood. Is it a temporary reaction to something specific, or has it been lingering? The duration of your mood can give you

insight into its seriousness and whether it may be a symptom of a deeper issue.

4. **Evaluate the Impact:** Analyze how this mood is affecting your behavior, relationships, and spiritual life. Are you withdrawing from others? Are you neglecting your responsibilities or spiritual disciplines? Understanding the impact of your mood can motivate you to take steps toward healing.
5. **Consult Scripture and Prayer:** Bring your mood before God in prayer, asking for wisdom and insight. James 1:5 assures us, "If any of you lacks wisdom, let him ask God, who gives generously to all without reproach, and it will be given him." Prayerfully seek God's guidance in understanding your mood and its implications.

Understanding the Spiritual Significance of Moods

Moods are not merely psychological phenomena; they also have spiritual significance. The Bible acknowledges the influence of moods and emotions on our spiritual life and encourages us to submit these aspects of our being to God. Galatians 5:22-23 speaks of the fruit of the Spirit, which includes qualities such as peace, joy, and self-control. These are not merely emotional states but evidence of the Holy Spirit's work in our lives.

However, when our moods are not in alignment with the fruit of the Spirit, they can hinder our spiritual growth and our relationship with God. For example, a prolonged mood of despair can lead to doubt in God's goodness, while persistent anger can harden the heart and lead to bitterness. Recognizing the spiritual dimension of your moods is essential for addressing them in a way that honors God.

In Ephesians 4:26-27, Paul warns, "Be angry and do not sin; do not let the sun go down on your anger, and give no opportunity to the devil." This passage highlights the danger of allowing moods, particularly negative ones, to linger unchecked. Unaddressed moods can give the enemy a foothold in your life, leading to further spiritual and emotional turmoil.

Practical Strategies for Managing and Transforming Moods

Once you have diagnosed your mood, the next step is to manage it in a way that promotes healing and spiritual growth. This process involves both spiritual disciplines and practical actions that help to transform your mood and bring it into alignment with God's will.

One effective strategy is to engage in regular prayer and meditation on Scripture. When you recognize a negative mood, take it to God in prayer, asking for His help to overcome it. As previously discussed, prayer should be paired with action. If you're struggling with a mood of anxiety, for instance, meditate on Scriptures that speak to God's peace, such as Philippians 4:6-7: "Do not be anxious about anything, but in everything by prayer and supplication with thanksgiving let your requests be made known to God. And the peace of God, which surpasses all understanding, will guard your hearts and your minds in Christ Jesus."

In addition to prayer, consider practical actions that address the root cause of your mood. If your mood is triggered by a lack of rest, prioritize getting adequate sleep and relaxation. If it's caused by unresolved conflict, seek reconciliation with the person involved. Taking these practical steps is an essential part of working on behalf of your prayers, as it demonstrates your commitment to aligning your life with God's truth.

Another powerful tool for managing moods is gratitude. A mood of discontentment or irritability can often be transformed by focusing on the blessings in your life. 1 Thessalonians 5:18 encourages us to "give thanks in all circumstances; for this is the will of God in Christ Jesus for you." Practicing gratitude shifts your perspective and helps to counteract negative moods by reminding you of God's goodness and faithfulness.

Physical activity can also play a role in managing moods. Exercise has been shown to have a positive impact on mental health, releasing endorphins that can improve your mood. Consider incorporating regular physical activity into your routine as a way to help stabilize your mood and enhance your overall well-being.

Finally, seeking support from others is crucial. Ecclesiastes 4:9-10 reminds us, "Two are better than one, because they have a good reward for their toil. For if they fall, one will lift up his fellow." Don't hesitate to reach out to a trusted friend, mentor, or counselor when you're struggling with a particular mood. They can offer encouragement, perspective, and prayer support, helping you to navigate your emotional challenges more effectively.

The Role of Ongoing Reflection and Adjustment

Diagnosing and managing your moods is not a one-time event but an ongoing process. As you grow in self-awareness and spiritual maturity, you will need to continually reflect on your emotional state and make adjustments as necessary. This ongoing reflection helps to prevent negative moods from taking root and allows you to live more fully in the freedom and peace that God offers.

Regularly take time to assess your moods and their triggers. Are there patterns that you notice? Are certain situations or thoughts consistently leading to negative moods? By identifying these patterns, you can take proactive steps to address them before they escalate.

Remember to incorporate prayer into this process, asking God to reveal any areas of your life that may be contributing to unhealthy moods. Psalm 19:12-13 is a powerful prayer for this purpose: "Who can discern his errors? Declare me innocent from hidden faults. Keep back your servant also from presumptuous sins; let them not have dominion over me! Then I shall be blameless, and innocent of great transgression." Allow God to search your heart and reveal any hidden issues that may be affecting your emotional state.

As you continue to grow in your ability to diagnose and manage your moods, you will find that your emotional life becomes more stable and aligned with God's will. This not only enhances your personal well-being but also deepens your relationship with God and others, allowing you to live out your faith with greater joy and effectiveness.

CHAPTER 8 How Can You Be Transformed by the Renewal of Your Mind and Keep It Renewed?

The transformation of the mind is at the core of Christian discipleship and personal growth. The Apostle Paul, in Romans 12:2, provides a pivotal command for believers: "Do not be conformed to this world, but be transformed by the renewal of your mind, that by testing you may discern what is the will of God, what is good and acceptable and perfect." This renewal is not a one-time event but an ongoing process that involves consistent effort, self-examination, and reliance on God's Word. Understanding how to renew your mind and maintain this renewed state is crucial for living a life that aligns with God's will and reflects His character. In this chapter, we will explore the process of mind renewal, the importance of maintaining a renewed mind, and practical strategies for ensuring that your thoughts remain aligned with biblical truth.

Understanding the Transformation Through Mind Renewal

The concept of mind renewal is deeply rooted in the recognition that our natural ways of thinking are often tainted by sin, shaped by the world's values, and influenced by past experiences that may not align with God's truth. The Bible consistently contrasts the wisdom of the world with the wisdom of God, urging believers to reject worldly thinking and embrace a mindset grounded in Scripture. Proverbs 3:5-6 offers this guidance: "Trust in Jehovah with all your heart, and do not lean on your own understanding. In all your ways acknowledge him, and he will make straight your paths." This passage highlights the importance of relying on God's wisdom rather than our own flawed understanding.

Mind renewal is about more than just acquiring new information; it involves a deep, spiritual transformation that affects every aspect of your life. The Greek word for "transformed" used in Romans 12:2 is *metamorphoō*, the same word used to describe Jesus' transfiguration in Matthew 17:2. This indicates a profound change from the inside out—a transformation that impacts your attitudes, desires, and behaviors.

The process of renewing your mind begins with recognizing the areas of your thinking that are out of alignment with God's truth. These areas might include negative thought patterns, misconceptions about God, or beliefs that contradict Scripture. Ephesians 4:22-24 encourages believers to "put off your old self, which belongs to your former manner of life and is corrupt through deceitful desires, and to be renewed in the spirit of your minds, and to put on the new self, created after the likeness of God in true righteousness and holiness." This passage underscores the need to discard old, sinful ways of thinking and embrace a new mindset that reflects God's righteousness.

The Process of Renewing Your Mind: A Practical Approach

Renewing your mind is an active and intentional process that requires both spiritual discipline and practical action. The first step in this process is to immerse yourself in God's Word. Psalm 119:11 says, "I have stored up your word in my heart, that I might not sin against you." Regularly reading, meditating on, and memorizing Scripture is essential for aligning your thoughts with God's truth. When you encounter thoughts or beliefs that contradict Scripture, you must replace them with the truth found in God's Word.

For instance, if you struggle with anxiety about the future, you might be inclined to focus on worst-case scenarios or to assume that things will never improve. These thoughts can be deeply ingrained and may feel overwhelming. However, renewing your mind involves identifying these anxious thoughts and replacing them with biblical truths. Philippians 4:6-7 offers a powerful alternative: "Do not be anxious about anything, but in everything by prayer and supplication with thanksgiving let your requests be made known to God. And the peace of God, which surpasses all understanding, will guard your hearts and your minds in Christ Jesus." By meditating on and internalizing this passage, you can begin to shift your focus from anxiety to trust in God's provision and peace.

Prayer is another crucial component of mind renewal. In prayer, you can ask God to reveal any areas of your thinking that need transformation and to help you internalize His truth. James 1:5 encourages believers to seek God's wisdom: "If any of you lacks wisdom, let him ask God, who gives generously to all without reproach, and it will be given him." In addition to praying for wisdom, it's important to pray specifically for the renewal of your mind, asking God to help you think in ways that honor Him and reflect His character.

It's also essential to guard your mind against influences that can lead you away from God's truth. This might involve being selective about the media you consume, the conversations you engage in, or the environments you place yourself in. Proverbs 4:23 provides this wisdom: "Keep your heart with all vigilance, for from it flow the springs of life." Being vigilant about what you allow into your mind is a critical part of maintaining a renewed mindset.

Furthermore, surrounding yourself with a community of believers who encourage and support your spiritual growth is vital. Proverbs 27:17 says, "Iron sharpens iron, and one man sharpens another." Engaging in fellowship with others who are committed to living according to God's Word can help you stay accountable in your journey of mind renewal. This community can provide you with encouragement, wisdom, and perspective as you seek to align your thoughts with Scripture.

Maintaining a Renewed Mind: Strategies for Long-Term Transformation

The ongoing renewal of your mind requires consistent effort and intentionality. One of the most effective ways to maintain a renewed mind is through regular self-examination and reflection. Lamentations 3:40 urges, "Let us test and examine our ways, and return to Jehovah!" Regularly assessing your thoughts and attitudes in light of Scripture helps to ensure that you are continually growing and transforming in your walk with God.

One practical strategy for maintaining a renewed mind is to establish a daily routine that includes time in God's Word and prayer. This routine could involve reading a passage of Scripture each morning, meditating on a verse throughout the day, and ending the day with prayer and reflection. By making this a daily practice, you ensure that your mind is consistently being renewed and aligned with God's truth.

Another important aspect of maintaining a renewed mind is to remain humble and teachable. Proverbs 3:7 warns, "Be not wise in your own eyes; fear Jehovah, and turn away from evil." Recognizing that your understanding is limited and that you are continually in need of God's guidance is key to ongoing transformation. Being open to correction and willing to adjust your thinking when confronted with Scripture is a sign of spiritual maturity and a critical component of keeping your mind renewed.

Additionally, it's important to apply God's truth in practical ways throughout your daily life. James 1:22-25 emphasizes the importance of being doers of the Word, not just hearers: "But be doers of the word, and not hearers only, deceiving yourselves. For if anyone is a hearer of the word and not a doer, he is like a man who looks intently at his natural face in a mirror. For he looks at himself and goes away and at once forgets what he was like. But the one who looks into the perfect law, the law of liberty, and perseveres, being no hearer who forgets but a doer who acts, he will be blessed in his doing." Applying what you learn from Scripture in practical ways solidifies the transformation of your mind and helps to ensure that your thoughts and actions are in harmony with God's will.

It's also beneficial to memorize and meditate on key Scriptures that address areas of your thinking that need continual renewal. For example, if you struggle with feelings of inadequacy, you might memorize Ephesians 2:10, which says, "For we are his workmanship, created in Christ Jesus for good works, which God prepared beforehand, that we should walk in them." Meditating on this verse can help to combat thoughts of inadequacy and remind you of your identity and purpose in Christ.

Another vital strategy for maintaining a renewed mind is to stay vigilant in prayer. Prayer should not be a one-time act but a continuous conversation with God, where you seek His guidance, confess areas where your mind may be drifting from His truth, and ask for the strength to remain aligned with His will. In Colossians 4:2, Paul exhorts believers to "Continue steadfastly in prayer, being watchful in it with thanksgiving." This steadfastness in prayer is essential for keeping your mind focused on God and His truth.

Addressing Challenges in Keeping the Mind Renewed

Despite your best efforts, there will be challenges and obstacles in maintaining a renewed mind. The world, the flesh, and the enemy will all attempt to draw your thoughts away from God's truth and back into old patterns of thinking. Recognizing these challenges and developing strategies to overcome them is crucial for long-term success.

One common challenge is the influence of the surrounding culture, which often promotes values and ideas that are contrary to Scripture. Romans 8:5-6 contrasts those who live according to the flesh with those who live according to the Spirit: "For those who live according to the flesh set their minds on the things of the flesh, but those who live according to the Spirit set their minds on the things of the Spirit. For to set the mind on the flesh is death, but to set the mind on the Spirit is life and peace." To counteract the influence of the world, it's important to be intentional about setting your mind on the things of the Spirit, which includes immersing yourself in Scripture, prayer, and fellowship with other believers.

Another challenge is the internal battle against sinful desires and thoughts. Galatians 5:16-17 highlights this struggle: "But I say, walk by the Spirit, and you will not gratify the desires of the flesh. For the desires of the flesh are against the Spirit, and the desires of the Spirit are against the flesh, for these are opposed to each other, to keep you from doing the things you want to do." To overcome this challenge, it's essential to rely on the Holy Spirit's power and continually surrender your thoughts and desires to God.

Discouragement can also be a significant obstacle in the process of mind renewal, especially when you feel like you're not making progress or when you fall back into old thought patterns. During these times, it's important to remind yourself of God's grace and to persevere in the process. Philippians 1:6 offers encouragement: "And I am sure of this, that he who began a good work in you will bring it to completion at the day of Jesus Christ." Trust that God is faithful to complete the work He has started in you, even when the journey is difficult.

Finally, it's important to remember that mind renewal is a lifelong process. As you grow in your relationship with God, you will continue to discover areas of your thinking that need transformation. Approach this process with patience and persistence, knowing that each step you take brings you closer to living in alignment with God's will.

CHAPTER 9 How Can You Build Self-Esteem and Embrace Your God-Given Potential?

Building self-esteem from a biblical perspective is about recognizing and embracing the value and identity that God has given you. It is not rooted in pride or self-exaltation, but in a humble acknowledgment of who you are in Christ and what you are capable of through His strength. The world often defines self-esteem as confidence in one's own abilities, looks, or achievements, but biblical self-esteem is grounded in the understanding that your worth comes from being made in the image of God and being loved and redeemed by Him. This chapter will explore how to build healthy self-esteem by aligning your thoughts and actions with God's truth, recognizing your God-given potential, and taking practical steps to grow in confidence and purpose.

Understanding Biblical Self-Esteem: Your Worth in God's Eyes

To build healthy self-esteem, you must first understand your intrinsic worth as a creation of God. Genesis 1:27 declares, "So God created man in his own image, in the image of God he created him; male and female he created them." This foundational truth establishes that every person is created in the image of God, which is the source of their inherent value. Your worth is not determined by external factors such as appearance, accomplishments, or social status, but by the fact that you are a reflection of God's character and creativity.

Furthermore, the Bible teaches that your worth is affirmed through the sacrificial love of Jesus Christ. Romans 5:8 emphasizes,

"But God shows his love for us in that while we were still sinners, Christ died for us." The fact that Christ gave His life to redeem you underscores your immense value in God's eyes. This understanding forms the foundation of biblical self-esteem—it is rooted not in self-reliance but in the recognition of God's love and the identity He has given you.

However, it's important to recognize that the fall of humanity introduced sin, which distorts self-perception. Many people struggle with feelings of inadequacy, shame, or worthlessness as a result of sin's impact on the world. These feelings are compounded by societal pressures and unrealistic expectations that can cause individuals to compare themselves to others and feel like they don't measure up. Ephesians 2:10 provides a powerful counter to these negative thoughts: "For we are his workmanship, created in Christ Jesus for good works, which God prepared beforehand, that we should walk in them." This verse reminds you that you are God's masterpiece, created with a unique purpose and equipped for good works that bring glory to Him.

Recognizing and Countering Negative Self-Perceptions

Negative self-perceptions often arise from a combination of past experiences, societal pressures, and spiritual warfare. These perceptions can manifest in various forms, such as self-doubt, fear of failure, or feelings of unworthiness. To build healthy self-esteem, it is essential to recognize and counter these negative thoughts with the truth of God's Word.

One common negative perception is the belief that you are not good enough or that you don't measure up to others. This mindset can lead to feelings of inadequacy and prevent you from pursuing your God-given potential. However, 2 Corinthians 3:5 offers reassurance: "Not that we are sufficient in ourselves to claim anything as coming from us, but our sufficiency is from God." This verse shifts the focus from self-reliance to reliance on God's sufficiency. Your worth and abilities are not dependent on your own strength but on the power and grace of God working through you.

Another negative perception is the fear of failure, which can paralyze you and prevent you from taking risks or pursuing your calling. This fear often stems from a desire for perfection or a fear of disappointing others. Proverbs 24:16 provides a biblical perspective on failure: "For the righteous falls seven times and rises again, but the wicked stumble in times of calamity." This verse emphasizes that failure is not the end but an opportunity for growth and perseverance. Building self-esteem involves embracing the possibility of failure as part of the learning process and trusting that God will give you the strength to rise again.

Feelings of unworthiness or shame can also undermine self-esteem, leading to a sense of hopelessness or despair. These feelings may be rooted in past sins, mistakes, or wounds from others. Yet, the Bible offers a message of redemption and restoration. Isaiah 43:1 proclaims, "Fear not, for I have redeemed you; I have called you by name, you are mine." God's redemption means that you are not defined by your past but by His grace and love. Building self-esteem requires accepting God's forgiveness and embracing your identity as His beloved child.

Practical Steps to Build and Strengthen Your Self-Esteem

Building self-esteem is not just about changing your thoughts but also about taking practical steps that reinforce your God-given identity and potential. These steps involve both spiritual disciplines and actionable behaviors that help you grow in confidence and purpose.

One of the most important steps in building self-esteem is immersing yourself in Scripture. The Bible is filled with passages that affirm your worth and identity in Christ. Regularly reading, meditating on, and memorizing these verses helps to renew your mind and counteract negative self-perceptions. Romans 12:2 encourages, "Do not be conformed to this world, but be transformed by the renewal of your mind, that by testing you may discern what is the will of God, what is good and acceptable and perfect." Renewing your mind with God's Word is foundational to building and maintaining healthy self-esteem.

In addition to engaging with Scripture, it's important to cultivate a strong prayer life. Prayer is not only a way to communicate with God but also a means of aligning your heart and mind with His truth. When you struggle with self-esteem, bring your concerns and insecurities before God in prayer. Ask Him to reveal any lies you've believed about yourself and to replace them with His truth. Philippians 4:6-7 provides comfort: "Do not be anxious about anything, but in everything by prayer and supplication with thanksgiving let your requests be made known to God. And the peace of God, which surpasses all understanding, will guard your hearts and your minds in Christ Jesus." Through prayer, you can experience God's peace and gain a clearer understanding of your worth in His eyes.

Another practical step is to set achievable goals that reflect your values and calling. Setting goals gives you a sense of purpose and direction, helping you to focus on what God has called you to do rather than comparing yourself to others. When setting goals, consider what talents and abilities God has given you and how you can use them to serve Him and others. Colossians 3:23 advises, "Whatever you do, work heartily, as for the Lord and not for men." By focusing on serving God in all that you do, you can build self-esteem that is grounded in fulfilling your divine purpose.

Taking care of your physical health is also an important aspect of building self-esteem. Your body is a temple of the Holy Spirit (1 Corinthians 6:19-20), and caring for it through proper nutrition, exercise, and rest can positively impact your self-perception. When you feel physically healthy and strong, you are better equipped to face challenges and pursue your goals with confidence. Additionally, engaging in physical activity can boost your mood and reduce stress, further enhancing your sense of well-being.

Building self-esteem also involves surrounding yourself with supportive and encouraging relationships. Proverbs 27:17 states, "Iron sharpens iron, and one man sharpens another." Being in community with other believers who affirm your worth and encourage you in your walk with God is vital for maintaining healthy self-esteem. Seek out relationships where you can give and receive encouragement, accountability, and love.

It's also essential to practice self-compassion. Many people are their own harshest critics, focusing on their flaws and failures rather than acknowledging their strengths and successes. Self-compassion involves treating yourself with the same kindness and understanding that you would offer to a friend. This doesn't mean excusing sin or ignoring areas where you need to grow, but it does mean recognizing that you are a work in progress and that God's grace is sufficient for your journey. Lamentations 3:22-23 reminds us, "The steadfast love of Jehovah never ceases; his mercies never come to an end; they are new every morning; great is your faithfulness." Embracing God's mercy and extending it to yourself is a key component of building self-esteem.

Overcoming Obstacles to Building Self-Esteem

Building self-esteem is a process that may involve overcoming various obstacles, such as past wounds, negative self-talk, and societal pressures. These challenges can be significant, but with God's help and practical strategies, they can be overcome.

Past wounds, such as rejection, betrayal, or abuse, can leave deep scars that affect your self-esteem. Healing from these wounds requires acknowledging the pain and bringing it before God for healing. Psalm 34:18 offers comfort: "Jehovah is near to the brokenhearted and saves the crushed in spirit." God is close to those who are hurting, and He offers healing and restoration. Seeking counseling or talking with a trusted mentor can also be valuable in processing past hurts and moving forward.

Negative self-talk is another common obstacle to building self-esteem. This inner dialogue often reinforces feelings of inadequacy or failure. To overcome negative self-talk, it's important to identify and challenge these thoughts with the truth of Scripture. For example, if you find yourself thinking, "I'm not capable of doing this," counter that thought with Philippians 4:13: "I can do all things through him who strengthens me." By consistently replacing negative thoughts with

God's truth, you can transform your inner dialogue and build a healthier self-perception.

Societal pressures can also impact self-esteem, especially when it comes to unrealistic standards of beauty, success, or achievement. The world often promotes a false image of what it means to be valuable or successful, leading many to feel like they don't measure up. Romans 12:2 warns against conforming to the patterns of this world, reminding us that true transformation comes from renewing our minds with God's truth. Building self-esteem involves rejecting worldly standards and embracing the identity and purpose that God has given you.

Embracing Your God-Given Potential

Ultimately, building self-esteem is about recognizing and embracing the potential that God has placed within you. Each person has been uniquely gifted and called by God to fulfill a specific purpose. Ephesians 2:10 affirms, "For we are his workmanship, created in Christ Jesus for good works, which God prepared beforehand, that we should walk in them." Embracing your potential means acknowledging your gifts, talents, and abilities as God-given and using them to serve Him and others.

As you grow in self-esteem, you will become more confident in stepping into the roles and opportunities that God has for you. This confidence is not based on pride or self-reliance, but on the assurance that God has equipped you for every good work. 2 Timothy 1:7 reminds us, "For God gave us a spirit not of fear but of power and love and self-control." With this assurance, you can pursue your calling with boldness and humility, knowing that God is with you every step of the way.

Building self-esteem is a journey that involves aligning your thoughts, actions, and attitudes with God's truth. By embracing your worth in God's eyes, countering negative self-perceptions, taking practical steps to grow in confidence, and overcoming obstacles, you can develop a healthy self-esteem that reflects your God-given identity and potential. This journey is not just about feeling better about yourself; it's about living fully in the purpose and calling that God has for you, bringing glory to Him in all that you do.

CHAPTER 10 How Can You Walk the Path to Behavioral Change?

Behavioral change is a fundamental aspect of spiritual growth and personal development. As believers, we are called not only to renew our minds but also to translate that renewal into tangible actions that reflect our faith and obedience to God. The path to behavioral change involves a deep commitment to aligning our actions with biblical principles, a recognition of the areas in our lives that need transformation, and the perseverance to make lasting changes that honor God. This chapter will explore the biblical foundation for behavioral change, the steps necessary to initiate and sustain it, and practical strategies for overcoming obstacles along the way.

The Biblical Foundation for Behavioral Change: Aligning Actions with Faith

Behavioral change is not just about modifying external actions but about a profound transformation that starts from within and manifests in every aspect of our lives. The Bible consistently emphasizes the importance of aligning our actions with our faith, illustrating that true faith is evidenced by the way we live. James 2:26 asserts, "For as the body apart from the spirit is dead, so also faith apart from works is dead." This passage underscores the necessity of actions that correspond to our beliefs, indicating that a faith that does not produce behavioral change is incomplete.

The call to behavioral change is rooted in the desire to reflect the character of Christ in our daily lives. Ephesians 4:22-24 instructs believers to "put off your old self, which belongs to your former manner of life and is corrupt through deceitful desires, and to be renewed in the spirit of your minds, and to put on the new self, created after the likeness of God in true righteousness and holiness." This process of putting off the old self and putting on the new self is a continual one, requiring daily commitment and the power of the Holy Spirit to guide us.

One of the key aspects of behavioral change is the recognition that it is not something we accomplish on our own. While our efforts are important, it is ultimately God who brings about true transformation. Philippians 2:13 reminds us, "For it is God who works in you, both to will and to work for his good pleasure." This verse highlights the divine partnership in the process of behavioral change—God provides the desire and the ability to change, while we respond in obedience to His leading.

Steps to Initiating Behavioral Change: A Practical Approach

Initiating behavioral change requires a clear understanding of the areas in your life that need transformation and a willingness to take actionable steps toward that change. The first step in this process is self-examination, where you honestly assess your behavior in light of Scripture. Psalm 139:23-24 is a powerful prayer for this purpose: "Search me, O God, and know my heart! Try me and know my thoughts! And see if there be any grievous way in me, and lead me in the way everlasting!" Inviting God to reveal areas of your life that need change is the foundation for effective transformation.

Once you have identified the behaviors that need to change, the next step is to set specific, achievable goals that align with biblical principles. These goals should be clear and measurable, providing a roadmap for the changes you want to make. For example, if you struggle with anger, a goal might be to practice patience and respond calmly in situations that typically trigger frustration. Proverbs 16:32 highlights the value of self-control: "Whoever is slow to anger is better than the mighty, and he who rules his spirit than he who takes a city." Setting goals based on Scripture helps ensure that your efforts are aligned with God's will.

Prayer is an essential component of initiating behavioral change. As you set your goals, bring them before God in prayer, asking for His guidance, strength, and wisdom. James 1:5 encourages believers to seek God's wisdom: "If any of you lacks wisdom, let him ask God, who gives generously to all without reproach, and it will be given him." Prayer should also include asking for the Holy Spirit's help in maintaining the changes you desire to make. Galatians 5:22-23 lists self-control as a fruit of the Spirit, indicating that our ability to change and sustain new behaviors is dependent on the Spirit's work in our lives.

In addition to prayer, it's important to develop a plan for how you will implement the changes you want to make. This plan should include practical steps that you can take on a daily basis. For instance, if your goal is to spend more time in God's Word, your plan might include setting aside a specific time each day for Bible study and meditation. Psalm 1:2-3 describes the blessed person whose "delight is in the law of Jehovah, and on his law he meditates day and night. He is like a tree planted by streams of water that yields its fruit in its season, and its leaf does not wither. In all that he does, he prospers." Establishing a consistent routine helps to reinforce new behaviors and ensures that you are regularly feeding your mind and spirit with God's truth.

Sustaining Behavioral Change: Perseverance and Spiritual Discipline

Sustaining behavioral change requires perseverance, especially when faced with challenges and setbacks. The Bible is clear that the Christian life involves ongoing effort and endurance. Hebrews 12:1-2 exhorts believers, "Therefore, since we are surrounded by so great a cloud of witnesses, let us also lay aside every weight, and sin which clings so closely, and let us run with endurance the race that is set before us, looking to Jesus, the founder and perfecter of our faith." This passage encourages us to stay focused on Christ as we pursue behavioral change, knowing that He is the source of our strength and the one who perfects our faith.

One of the most effective ways to sustain behavioral change is through the practice of spiritual disciplines. These disciplines, such as prayer, Bible study, fasting, and fellowship, help to cultivate a deeper relationship with God and provide the spiritual nourishment needed to maintain new behaviors. 1 Timothy 4:7-8 emphasizes the value of spiritual discipline: "Have nothing to do with irreverent, silly myths. Rather train yourself for godliness; for while bodily training is of some value, godliness is of value in every way, as it holds promise for the present life and also for the life to come." Regularly engaging in spiritual disciplines strengthens your resolve and helps you to stay committed to the changes you have made.

Accountability is another crucial element in sustaining behavioral change. Proverbs 27:17 states, "Iron sharpens iron, and one man sharpens another." Being accountable to a trusted friend, mentor, or small group provides encouragement, support, and a sense of responsibility. When you know that others are aware of your goals and are praying for you, it can motivate you to stay on track and continue making progress. Additionally, having someone to share your struggles and successes with can help to reinforce your commitment to change.

It's also important to celebrate the progress you make along the way. Acknowledging the milestones you reach, no matter how small, helps to build momentum and encourages you to keep moving forward. Psalm 126:3 declares, "Jehovah has done great things for us; we are glad." Recognizing God's work in your life and giving Him praise for the changes He has brought about fosters a spirit of gratitude and keeps your focus on His faithfulness.

Overcoming Obstacles to Behavioral Change

While the path to behavioral change is rewarding, it is not without its challenges. Obstacles such as temptation, discouragement, and spiritual warfare can threaten to derail your progress. Recognizing these obstacles and developing strategies to overcome them is essential for long-term success.

Temptation is one of the most common obstacles to behavioral change. The Bible teaches that temptation is a part of the human experience but provides reassurance that God will not allow you to be tempted beyond your ability to resist. 1 Corinthians 10:13 offers this promise: "No temptation has overtaken you that is not common to man. God is faithful, and he will not let you be tempted beyond your ability, but with the temptation he will also provide the way of escape, that you may be able to endure it." When faced with temptation, it's important to rely on God's strength and seek the way of escape that He provides. This may involve removing yourself from a tempting situation, turning to Scripture for encouragement, or reaching out to someone for support.

Discouragement is another obstacle that can hinder behavioral change, especially when progress seems slow or setbacks occur. It's important to remember that change is often a gradual process and that setbacks do not define your journey. Galatians 6:9 encourages perseverance: "And let us not grow weary of doing good, for in due season we will reap, if we do not give up." When you feel discouraged, take time to reflect on the progress you have made and remind yourself of God's promises. Prayer, reflection on Scripture, and seeking encouragement from others can help to renew your resolve and keep you moving forward.

Spiritual warfare is a reality that every believer must contend with. The enemy seeks to discourage, distract, and derail your efforts to change, but the Bible provides assurance that you can stand firm against his attacks. Ephesians 6:10-11 instructs, "Finally, be strong in the Lord and in the strength of his might. Put on the whole armor of God, that you may be able to stand against the schemes of the devil." Engaging in spiritual warfare through prayer, the Word of God, and reliance on the Holy Spirit equips you to resist the enemy's attacks and continue on the path to behavioral change.

Another important aspect of overcoming obstacles is recognizing the need for God's grace. No matter how committed you are to change, there will be times when you fall short. In these moments, it's crucial to remember that God's grace is sufficient for you, and His power is made perfect in weakness (2 Corinthians 12:9). Confess your shortcomings to God, receive His forgiveness, and ask for the strength to continue on the path of transformation.

Practical Strategies for Behavioral Change

In addition to spiritual disciplines, there are practical strategies you can implement to support your efforts in behavioral change. One such strategy is to create an environment that supports your goals. This might involve removing distractions or triggers that lead to negative behaviors, organizing your space to promote positive habits, or surrounding yourself with reminders of your goals. For example, if your goal is to spend more time in prayer, you might create a designated prayer space in your home where you can focus without interruptions.

Another strategy is to develop new habits that reinforce the changes you want to make. Habits are powerful because they automate behaviors, making it easier to maintain new actions over time. James Clear, in his book *Atomic Habits*, emphasizes the importance of making small, consistent changes that compound over time. While this is not a biblical text, the principle of gradual growth aligns with the biblical concept of perseverance and the importance of building on small victories. Consider starting with small, manageable changes that you can build upon as you progress.

It's also helpful to regularly review and adjust your goals and strategies as needed. Life circumstances, challenges, and opportunities change over time, and your approach to behavioral change may need to adapt accordingly. Proverbs 16:9 reminds us, "The heart of man plans his way, but Jehovah establishes his steps." Be open to God's leading and willing to adjust your plans as He directs.

Finally, consider the impact of your behavior on others. Behavioral change is not just about personal growth but also about how your actions affect those around you. Matthew 5:16 encourages us to "let your light shine before others, so that they may see your good works and give glory to your Father who is in heaven." As you pursue behavioral change, consider how your actions can be a testimony to God's work in your life and an encouragement to others.

The Journey of Behavioral Change: A Lifelong Commitment

Behavioral change is not a destination but a journey that requires ongoing commitment, perseverance, and reliance on God's grace. As you walk this path, remember that true transformation comes from the Holy Spirit working in you, enabling you to live a life that honors God and reflects His character. Philippians 1:6 provides encouragement: "And I am sure of this, that he who began a good work in you will bring it to completion at the day of Jesus Christ." Trust that God is faithful to complete the work He has started in you, and continue to seek His guidance, strength, and wisdom as you pursue behavioral change.

CHAPTER 11 How to Break Out of a Bad Mood

Bad moods are a common experience that can arise from various triggers, including stress, unmet expectations, interpersonal conflicts, or even physical factors like fatigue or hunger. While it's normal to experience bad moods from time to time, allowing them to linger can lead to negative consequences for your spiritual, emotional, and relational well-being. The Bible addresses the importance of maintaining a joyful spirit and offers wisdom on how to overcome negative emotions. This chapter explores how to break out of a bad mood through a combination of spiritual principles, practical actions, and the renewal of your mind.

Recognizing the Source of Your Bad Mood: A Spiritual and Practical Assessment

Before you can effectively break out of a bad mood, it's important to recognize its source. Bad moods can stem from a variety of causes, and understanding the root of your feelings is the first step toward addressing them. Proverbs 4:23 advises, "Keep your heart with all vigilance, for from it flow the springs of life." This verse highlights the importance of guarding your heart and being aware of the emotions that influence your thoughts and actions.

One common source of bad moods is unmet expectations. When reality doesn't align with your hopes or desires, it can lead to feelings of frustration, disappointment, or anger. These emotions, if not addressed, can quickly spiral into a negative mood that affects your entire day. James 4:1-3 provides insight into the role of desires in causing conflicts and negative emotions: "What causes quarrels and what causes fights among you? Is it not this, that your passions are at war within you? You desire and do not have, so you murder. You covet and cannot obtain, so you fight and quarrel. You do not have, because you do not ask. You ask and do not receive, because you ask wrongly, to spend it on your passions." Recognizing when unmet expectations are the cause of your bad mood allows you to bring those desires before God and seek His guidance on how to align your will with His.

Another source of bad moods is interpersonal conflict. Disagreements, misunderstandings, or hurtful interactions with others can leave you feeling upset and emotionally drained. Ephesians 4:26-27 warns, "Be angry and do not sin; do not let the sun go down on your anger, and give no opportunity to the devil." This passage emphasizes the importance of addressing negative emotions before they have a chance to take root and cause further harm. When conflict is the source of your bad mood, it's essential to seek reconciliation and resolve the issue in a way that honors God.

Physical factors, such as lack of sleep, poor nutrition, or illness, can also contribute to bad moods. While these factors may seem unrelated to spiritual life, the Bible acknowledges the connection between physical well-being and emotional health. In 1 Kings 19:5-8, after the prophet Elijah fled from Jezebel and fell into a deep depression, God addressed his physical needs by providing food and rest before speaking to him. This account illustrates that caring for your body is an important part of maintaining emotional and spiritual well-being.

Shifting Your Focus: Redirecting Your Thoughts and Emotions

Once you've identified the source of your bad mood, the next step is to shift your focus and redirect your thoughts and emotions toward what is true, honorable, and praiseworthy. Philippians 4:8 provides a powerful guide for this process: "Finally, brothers, whatever is true, whatever is honorable, whatever is just, whatever is pure, whatever is lovely, whatever is commendable, if there is any excellence, if there is anything worthy of praise, think about these things." By intentionally focusing on positive and godly things, you can begin to lift your mood and realign your perspective with God's truth.

One effective way to shift your focus is through gratitude. Gratitude has the power to transform your mood by redirecting your attention from what is wrong to what is right in your life. 1 Thessalonians 5:18 encourages believers to "give thanks in all circumstances; for this is the will of God in Christ Jesus for you." Practicing gratitude involves taking time to reflect on the blessings you have received and expressing thanks to God for His goodness. This can be done through prayer, journaling, or simply speaking words of thanks throughout the day. As you cultivate a heart of gratitude, you will find that your mood begins to improve, and your outlook becomes more positive.

Another way to shift your focus is through worship. Worshiping God, whether through singing, reading Scripture, or meditating on His attributes, helps to elevate your thoughts and emotions above your current circumstances. Psalm 100:4-5 invites us to "Enter his gates with thanksgiving, and his courts with praise! Give thanks to him; bless his name! For Jehovah is good; his steadfast love endures forever, and his faithfulness to all generations." Worship not only honors God but also has the effect of lifting your spirit and restoring joy to your heart.

In addition to gratitude and worship, engaging in acts of kindness can also help to break a bad mood. Serving others and focusing on their needs can shift your attention away from your own negative feelings and bring a sense of fulfillment and purpose. Proverbs 11:25 states, "Whoever brings blessing will be enriched, and one who waters will himself be watered." By reaching out to others in love and service, you can experience the joy that comes from being a blessing to others.

Renewing Your Mind: Aligning Your Thoughts with God's Truth

Renewing your mind is a key component in breaking out of a bad mood. Negative thoughts and emotions often arise from patterns of thinking that are not aligned with God's truth. Romans 12:2 instructs, "Do not be conformed to this world, but be transformed by the renewal of your mind, that by testing you may discern what is the will of God, what is good and acceptable and perfect." The process of renewing your mind involves identifying and replacing distorted or negative thoughts with the truth of Scripture.

One practical way to renew your mind is by memorizing and meditating on specific Bible verses that address the issues you are facing. For example, if your bad mood is rooted in anxiety, you might meditate on Philippians 4:6-7, which reminds us not to be anxious but to bring our concerns to God in prayer, with the promise that His peace will guard our hearts and minds. If your mood is the result of feeling overwhelmed, you might turn to Psalm 61:2, which says, "From the end of the earth I call to you when my heart is faint. Lead me to the rock that is higher than I." By focusing on these verses, you allow God's truth to penetrate your mind and bring peace to your heart.

Another aspect of renewing your mind is reframing your perspective. Reframing involves looking at your situation from a different angle, particularly from a biblical viewpoint. For instance, instead of viewing a challenging circumstance as a burden, you can reframe it as an opportunity for growth and dependence on God. James 1:2-4 encourages this mindset: "Count it all joy, my brothers, when you meet trials of various kinds, for you know that the testing of your faith produces steadfastness. And let steadfastness have its full effect, that you may be perfect and complete, lacking in nothing." By reframing your situation, you can find purpose and meaning even in difficult times, which can help to lift your mood.

It's also helpful to practice self-compassion as you renew your mind. Many people are quick to criticize themselves when they are in a bad mood, which only serves to reinforce negative feelings. Instead, extend grace to yourself, recognizing that everyone experiences bad moods and that they do not define your worth or character. Lamentations 3:22-23 reminds us, "The steadfast love of Jehovah never ceases; his mercies never come to an end; they are new every morning; great is your faithfulness." Embrace God's mercy and allow it to renew your mind and heart.

Taking Action: Practical Steps to Overcome a Bad Mood

While renewing your mind and shifting your focus are essential, breaking out of a bad mood also requires practical action. Taking concrete steps to address the source of your mood and engage in activities that promote well-being can help to restore joy and peace.

One practical step is to engage in physical activity. Exercise has been shown to have a positive impact on mood by releasing endorphins, which are natural mood enhancers. 1 Timothy 4:8 acknowledges the value of physical training: "For while bodily training is of some value, godliness is of value in every way, as it holds promise for the present life and also for the life to come." Taking a walk, going for a run, or participating in a favorite physical activity can help to lift your spirits and improve your overall sense of well-being.

Another practical step is to spend time in nature. The beauty and tranquility of God's creation can have a calming and restorative effect on your mood. Psalm 19:1 declares, "The heavens declare the glory of God, and the sky above proclaims his handiwork." Spending time outdoors, whether in a park, garden, or natural setting, can help you to connect with God and experience His peace.

Social connection is also important in overcoming a bad mood. Reaching out to a trusted friend or family member for support, encouragement, or simply a listening ear can make a significant difference in how you feel. Ecclesiastes 4:9-10 emphasizes the value of companionship: "Two are better than one, because they have a good reward for their toil. For if they fall, one will lift up his fellow. But woe to him who is alone when he falls and has not another to lift him up!" Sharing your feelings with someone who cares can provide comfort and help to break the isolation that often accompanies a bad mood.

In addition to social connection, engaging in a creative activity can help to lift your mood. Whether it's drawing, writing, cooking, or playing an instrument, creative expression allows you to channel your emotions in a positive and productive way. Exodus 35:35 speaks of God giving people the skill to engage in creative work: "He has filled them with skill to do every sort of work done by an engraver or by a designer or by an embroiderer in blue and purple and scarlet yarns and fine twined linen, or by a weaver—by any sort of workman or skilled designer." Tapping into your creative abilities can bring a sense of accomplishment and joy.

Lastly, consider practicing deep breathing or relaxation techniques to help calm your mind and body. These techniques can help to reduce stress and anxiety, making it easier to shift out of a bad mood. Psalm 46:10 encourages us to "Be still, and know that I am God." Taking time to be still, breathe deeply, and focus on God's presence can bring peace to your soul and help to restore your mood.

Maintaining a Positive and Joyful Spirit

Breaking out of a bad mood is not just about finding temporary relief but about cultivating a positive and joyful spirit that endures. The Bible calls believers to live with joy, regardless of their circumstances. Philippians 4:4 exhorts, "Rejoice in the Lord always; again I will say, rejoice." This joy is not dependent on external factors but is rooted in your relationship with God and the assurance of His love and faithfulness.

To maintain a joyful spirit, it's important to cultivate habits that promote emotional and spiritual well-being. Regular time in prayer and Scripture, gratitude, worship, and fellowship with other believers are all essential practices that help to sustain joy. Nehemiah 8:10 reminds us, "The joy of Jehovah is your strength." By drawing on God's joy, you can navigate life's challenges with a resilient and positive spirit.

CHAPTER 12 Let All Wrath and Anger Be Put Away from Us

Wrath and anger are powerful emotions that, when left unchecked, can cause significant harm to both the individual harboring them and those around them. The Bible repeatedly warns against the dangers of wrath and anger, urging believers to put these emotions away and to cultivate a spirit of patience, forgiveness, and love. However, overcoming these emotions is not simply a matter of willpower; it requires deep spiritual transformation, practical strategies, and a commitment to living according to God's principles. This chapter explores the biblical teaching on wrath and anger, provides practical steps for overcoming these destructive emotions, and offers guidance on how to replace them with godly virtues.

Understanding the Dangers of Wrath and Anger: A Biblical Perspective

The Bible is clear about the dangers of wrath and anger, frequently linking these emotions to sin and discord. In Ephesians 4:31, Paul instructs believers, "Let all bitterness and wrath and anger and clamor and slander be put away from you, along with all malice." This verse encapsulates the biblical mandate to rid ourselves of these destructive emotions, recognizing that they can lead to behaviors and attitudes that are contrary to the spirit of Christ.

One of the primary reasons wrath and anger are so dangerous is that they can easily lead to sinful actions. James 1:19-20 advises, "Know this, my beloved brothers: let every person be quick to hear, slow to speak, slow to anger; for the anger of man does not produce the righteousness of God." Human anger, when not controlled, can result in rash decisions, hurtful words, and broken relationships. It is an emotion that often stems from pride, selfishness, or a sense of injustice, but instead of leading to righteous outcomes, it tends to escalate situations and cause further harm.

Moreover, the Bible warns that harboring wrath and anger can give the devil a foothold in your life. Ephesians 4:26-27 cautions, "Be angry and do not sin; do not let the sun go down on your anger, and give no opportunity to the devil." When anger is allowed to fester, it can open the door to bitterness, resentment, and other destructive emotions that can take root in the heart. This can create a spiritual stronghold that is difficult to break, leading to ongoing conflict and a separation from the peace of God.

Wrath and anger can also hinder your relationship with God. In Matthew 5:21-22, Jesus expands on the commandment against murder by addressing the heart attitude of anger: "You have heard that it was said to those of old, 'You shall not murder; and whoever murders will be liable to judgment.' But I say to you that everyone who is angry with his brother will be liable to judgment." Jesus teaches that anger, like murder, is subject to divine judgment because it reveals a heart that is not aligned with God's love and justice. This passage underscores the seriousness of anger and the need to address it at the heart level.

Recognizing the Roots of Wrath and Anger

To effectively put away wrath and anger, it is essential to recognize their roots. Anger often arises from a combination of unmet expectations, perceived injustices, and unresolved emotional pain. These factors can trigger a sense of frustration, helplessness, or indignation, leading to an outburst of anger. Proverbs 19:11 provides insight into the value of patience in the face of provocation: "Good sense makes one slow to anger, and it is his glory to overlook an offense." This verse suggests that the ability to overlook offenses and be slow to anger is a sign of wisdom and maturity.

One common root of anger is pride. When your pride is wounded, whether through insult, rejection, or criticism, it can lead to feelings of anger as a defense mechanism. Proverbs 16:18 warns, "Pride goes before destruction, and a haughty spirit before a fall." Recognizing pride as a root cause of anger allows you to address the underlying issue and cultivate humility, which can help to defuse anger before it takes hold.

Another root of anger is a sense of injustice. When you perceive that you or someone you care about has been wronged, it can trigger righteous indignation. While there is a place for righteous anger, the Bible warns against allowing it to lead to sin. Romans 12:19 instructs, "Beloved, never avenge yourselves, but leave it to the wrath of God, for it is written, 'Vengeance is mine, I will repay, says Jehovah.'" This verse reminds believers that it is God's role to execute justice, and we are called to trust in His judgment rather than take matters into our own hands.

Unresolved emotional pain is another significant root of anger. Past hurts, traumas, or disappointments can simmer beneath the surface and manifest as anger when triggered by current events. Psalm 147:3 offers hope for healing: "He heals the brokenhearted and binds up their wounds." Bringing these wounds before God in prayer and seeking His healing is crucial for overcoming anger that is rooted in past pain.

Practical Steps to Overcome Wrath and Anger

Overcoming wrath and anger requires both spiritual and practical strategies. The first step is to commit to regular self-examination and prayer, asking God to reveal any areas of your life where anger has taken root. Psalm 139:23-24 is a powerful prayer for this purpose: "Search me, O God, and know my heart! Try me and know my thoughts! And see if there be any grievous way in me, and lead me in the way everlasting!" By inviting God to search your heart, you open yourself to His guidance and correction.

Once you have identified the presence of wrath or anger in your life, the next step is to take practical measures to address it. One effective strategy is to practice delaying your response when you feel anger rising. Proverbs 14:29 teaches, "Whoever is slow to anger has great understanding, but he who has a hasty temper exalts folly." By taking time to pause, breathe, and pray before responding, you can prevent anger from leading to sinful actions or words.

Another important step is to cultivate forgiveness. Forgiveness is a powerful antidote to anger, as it releases the hold that past offenses have on your heart. Ephesians 4:32 instructs, "Be kind to one another, tenderhearted, forgiving one another, as God in Christ forgave you." Forgiving those who have wronged you is not only a command but also a way to free yourself from the burden of anger and bitterness. It's important to remember that forgiveness does not condone the wrong that was done, but it does release you from the desire for revenge and allows you to move forward in peace.

In addition to forgiveness, developing a habit of gratitude can help to counteract anger. Gratitude shifts your focus from what is wrong to what is right, helping to diffuse negative emotions. Colossians 3:15 encourages believers to "let the peace of Christ rule in your hearts, to which indeed you were called in one body. And be thankful." By regularly expressing thanks to God for His blessings, you can cultivate a heart of contentment that is less prone to anger.

It's also important to seek reconciliation when anger has caused conflict in your relationships. Matthew 5:23-24 emphasizes the importance of reconciliation: "So if you are offering your gift at the altar and there remember that your brother has something against you, leave your gift there before the altar and go. First be reconciled to your brother, and then come and offer your gift." Reconciliation involves taking responsibility for any harm you have caused, seeking forgiveness, and working to restore the relationship. This process not only honors God but also helps to heal the wounds that anger has inflicted.

Replacing Wrath and Anger with Godly Virtues

The goal of putting away wrath and anger is not just the absence of these emotions but the cultivation of godly virtues that reflect the character of Christ. As you work to overcome anger, it's important to actively pursue virtues such as patience, kindness, and self-control.

Patience is a key virtue in overcoming anger. James 1:19-20 advises, "Let every person be quick to hear, slow to speak, slow to anger; for the anger of man does not produce the righteousness of God." Patience involves giving others the benefit of the doubt, allowing time for emotions to settle before responding, and trusting in God's timing rather than demanding immediate resolution. Cultivating patience can help you to respond to difficult situations with grace rather than anger.

Kindness is another virtue that can counteract anger. Ephesians 4:32 encourages, "Be kind to one another, tenderhearted, forgiving one another, as God in Christ forgave you." Kindness involves showing compassion and understanding, even when others are difficult or unkind. By choosing to respond with kindness, you can break the cycle of anger and create an environment of peace and mutual respect.

Self-control is essential in managing anger. Galatians 5:22-23 lists self-control as a fruit of the Spirit, indicating that it is a quality that the Holy Spirit produces in believers. Practicing self-control means being intentional about your responses, choosing to act in ways that honor God rather than being driven by emotions. It also involves setting boundaries to prevent anger from escalating, such as walking away from a heated situation or taking time to cool down before addressing an issue.

Finally, love is the overarching virtue that encompasses all others. Colossians 3:14-15 instructs, "And above all these put on love, which binds everything together in perfect harmony. And let the peace of Christ rule in your hearts, to which indeed you were called in one body. And be thankful." Love is the antidote to anger because it seeks the good of others, even at the cost of your own pride or desires. By cultivating a heart of love, you can respond to challenges and offenses with grace, patience, and forgiveness.

Trusting in God's Justice and Sovereignty

One of the reasons anger can be so difficult to overcome is that it often stems from a sense of injustice or a desire for control. When things don't go as you think they should, or when you are wronged, it's natural to feel angry. However, the Bible calls believers to trust in God's justice and sovereignty rather than taking matters into their own hands.

Romans 12:19 provides a clear directive: "Beloved, never avenge yourselves, but leave it to the wrath of God, for it is written, 'Vengeance is mine, I will repay, says Jehovah.'" This verse reminds you that God is the ultimate judge, and He will bring justice in His time and in His way. Trusting in God's justice allows you to release your anger and leave the outcome in His hands.

Similarly, trusting in God's sovereignty means recognizing that He is in control of all circumstances, even those that provoke anger. Proverbs 3:5-6 advises, "Trust in Jehovah with all your heart, and do not lean on your own understanding. In all your ways acknowledge him, and he will make straight your paths." When you trust that God is sovereign and that He is working all things for your good, it becomes easier to let go of anger and respond with faith and patience.

Continual Growth in Overcoming Anger

Overcoming wrath and anger is not a one-time event but a continual process of growth and spiritual maturity. As you seek to put away these destructive emotions, it's important to remain vigilant in prayer, self-examination, and reliance on the Holy Spirit. Philippians 1:6 offers encouragement: "And I am sure of this, that he who began a good work in you will bring it to completion at the day of Jesus Christ." Trust that God is faithful to complete the work He has started in you and continue to pursue the virtues that reflect His character.

CHAPTER 13 How Can You Deal with Your Depression and Find Hope in God?

Depression is a deep and complex emotional struggle that affects many people, including Christians. It can manifest as a persistent feeling of sadness, hopelessness, and despair, often accompanied by physical symptoms like fatigue, changes in appetite, and difficulty concentrating. While the Bible acknowledges the reality of suffering and emotional pain, it also offers hope and guidance for those who are battling depression. This chapter will explore the biblical perspective on depression, the spiritual and practical steps you can take to address it, and how to find hope in God during times of darkness.

Understanding Depression: A Biblical Perspective on Emotional Suffering

Depression is not a new phenomenon; it is something that has afflicted people throughout history, including many of the faithful men and women in the Bible. The Scriptures do not shy away from depicting the emotional struggles of its characters, offering a raw and honest portrayal of their pain. For example, King David, a man after God's own heart, experienced deep bouts of depression, as evidenced in many of his psalms. In Psalm 42:5, David cries out, "Why are you cast down, O my soul, and why are you in turmoil within me? Hope in God; for I shall again praise him, my salvation." This verse captures the inner turmoil and the tension between despair and hope that often accompanies depression.

Similarly, the prophet Elijah, after his victory over the prophets of Baal, fell into a deep depression and even wished for death. In 1 Kings 19:4, Elijah says, "It is enough; now, O Jehovah, take away my life, for I am no better than my fathers." Despite his great faith and the mighty works he had accomplished, Elijah found himself overwhelmed by fear and despair, a reminder that even the most spiritually mature individuals can struggle with depression.

Job, too, is a biblical figure who experienced profound suffering and depression. After losing his children, wealth, and health, Job lamented his existence, saying in Job 3:26, "I am not at ease, nor am I quiet; I have no rest, but trouble comes." Job's story illustrates the depth of emotional pain that can accompany severe trials, yet it also demonstrates the importance of maintaining faith in God even when life feels unbearable.

These examples show that depression is not a sign of weak faith or a lack of spirituality. Rather, it is a part of the human experience in a fallen world, where suffering and pain are inevitable. The Bible offers comfort and hope to those who are struggling with depression, encouraging them to turn to God in their darkest moments and to trust in His unfailing love and mercy.

Recognizing the Signs of Depression: Spiritual and Practical Insights

Recognizing the signs of depression is the first step toward addressing it. Depression can manifest in various ways, including persistent sadness, feelings of hopelessness, loss of interest in activities that once brought joy, changes in sleep patterns, difficulty concentrating, and physical symptoms such as fatigue or changes in appetite. It is important to acknowledge these symptoms and not dismiss them as merely a passing mood.

The Bible encourages self-examination as a way to gain insight into one's emotional and spiritual state. Lamentations 3:40 advises, "Let us test and examine our ways, and return to Jehovah!" By taking time to reflect on your emotions and behaviors, you can identify patterns that may indicate depression and take steps to address them.

One of the challenges of depression is that it can distort your perception of reality, leading you to believe lies about yourself, others, and God. For example, you may feel that you are unworthy of love, that your situation is hopeless, or that God has abandoned you. These thoughts are not based on truth but on the lies of the enemy, who seeks to destroy your peace and joy. John 8:44 describes Satan as "a liar and the father of lies," emphasizing the importance of discerning truth from deception.

To combat these lies, it is essential to renew your mind with the truth of God's Word. Romans 12:2 instructs, "Do not be conformed to this world, but be transformed by the renewal of your mind, that by testing you may discern what is the will of God, what is good and acceptable and perfect." By immersing yourself in Scripture and meditating on God's promises, you can counter the lies of the enemy and replace them with the truth of who you are in Christ.

Spiritual and Practical Steps to Address Depression

Addressing depression requires a holistic approach that includes both spiritual and practical steps. While prayer and reliance on God are foundational, it is also important to take practical actions that support your mental and emotional well-being.

One of the most important spiritual practices in dealing with depression is prayer. Prayer is not just a means of asking God for help but also a way of pouring out your heart to Him and finding comfort in His presence. Psalm 34:17-18 offers reassurance: "When the righteous cry for help, Jehovah hears and delivers them out of all their troubles. Jehovah is near to the brokenhearted and saves the crushed in spirit." Bringing your pain, fears, and doubts to God in prayer allows you to experience His comfort and peace, even in the midst of suffering.

In addition to prayer, spending time in God's Word is crucial for overcoming depression. The Bible is filled with promises of God's love, faithfulness, and care, which can bring hope and encouragement to a weary soul. For example, Isaiah 41:10 reminds us, "Fear not, for I am with you; be not dismayed, for I am your God; I will strengthen you, I will help you, I will uphold you with my righteous right hand." Meditating on such verses can help to lift your spirits and restore your faith in God's goodness.

It is also important to cultivate gratitude, even in the midst of depression. Gratitude has the power to shift your focus from what is wrong to what is right, helping to combat the negative thought patterns that often accompany depression. Philippians 4:6-7 encourages believers to "do not be anxious about anything, but in everything by prayer and supplication with thanksgiving let your requests be made known to God. And the peace of God, which surpasses all understanding, will guard your hearts and your minds in Christ Jesus." By regularly expressing thanks to God for His blessings, you can begin to experience His peace and joy, even in difficult times.

Another practical step in addressing depression is to seek support from others. The Bible emphasizes the importance of community and fellowship, recognizing that believers are not meant to bear their burdens alone. Galatians 6:2 instructs, "Bear one another's burdens, and so fulfill the law of Christ." Reaching out to a trusted friend, pastor, or counselor can provide much-needed support, encouragement, and accountability. Talking about your struggles with someone who cares can help to alleviate the feelings of isolation and hopelessness that often accompany depression.

In addition to seeking support from others, it is important to take care of your physical health. Depression can have a significant impact on your body, leading to fatigue, changes in appetite, and other physical symptoms. Ensuring that you get enough sleep, eat a balanced diet, and engage in regular physical activity can help to improve your mood and energy levels. 1 Corinthians 6:19-20 reminds us, "Or do you not know that your body is a temple of the Holy Spirit within you, whom you have from God? You are not your own, for you were bought with a price. So glorify God in your body." Taking care of your body is an important aspect of honoring God and supporting your overall well-being.

Finding Hope in God: Trusting in His Faithfulness

One of the most difficult aspects of depression is the feeling of hopelessness that can accompany it. However, the Bible offers a message of hope that is not dependent on circumstances but is rooted in the unchanging character of God. Lamentations 3:21-23 declares, "But this I call to mind, and therefore I have hope: The steadfast love of Jehovah never ceases; his mercies never come to an end; they are new every morning; great is your faithfulness." This passage reminds us that no matter how dark things may seem, God's love and mercy are always present, offering new hope each day.

Trusting in God's faithfulness involves surrendering your fears, doubts, and pain to Him and believing that He is working all things for your good. Romans 8:28 assures us, "And we know that for those who love God all things work together for good, for those who are called according to his purpose." Even in the midst of depression, you can trust that God is with you and that He is using your suffering to accomplish His purposes in your life.

It is also important to remember that God understands your pain and is compassionate toward your struggles. Psalm 34:18 provides comfort: "Jehovah is near to the brokenhearted and saves the crushed in spirit." God is not distant or indifferent to your suffering; He is present with you in your pain and offers His comfort and peace.

Finally, finding hope in God involves looking beyond your current circumstances to the eternal hope that is found in Christ. 2 Corinthians 4:16-18 encourages believers to "not lose heart. Though our outer self is wasting away, our inner self is being renewed day by day. For this light momentary affliction is preparing for us an eternal weight of glory beyond all comparison, as we look not to the things that are seen but to the things that are unseen. For the things that are seen are transient, but the things that are unseen are eternal." This passage reminds us that our present suffering is temporary and that we have an eternal future with Christ that far outweighs any trials we may face in this life.

In conclusion, dealing with depression is a complex and challenging journey, but it is one that can be navigated with God's help. By recognizing the signs of depression, taking spiritual and practical steps to address it, and finding hope in God's faithfulness, you can overcome the darkness and experience the peace and joy that He offers.

CHAPTER 14 How Can You Play an Active Role in Managing Your Bipolar Disorder?

Bipolar disorder is a complex mental health condition characterized by extreme mood swings, including episodes of mania (or hypomania) and depression. These mood fluctuations can be challenging to manage, but with the right approach, individuals with bipolar disorder can live balanced and fulfilling lives. For Christians facing this condition, it is important to integrate faith with practical strategies to actively manage bipolar disorder. This chapter explores how to take an active role in managing bipolar disorder through spiritual practices, practical steps, and reliance on God's guidance.

Understanding Bipolar Disorder: A Biblical and Medical Perspective

Bipolar disorder is a medical condition that affects the brain's chemistry, leading to significant shifts in mood, energy levels, and behavior. These changes can be severe and may disrupt daily life, relationships, and overall well-being. While the Bible does not specifically mention bipolar disorder, it does acknowledge the reality of emotional and psychological struggles. Many biblical figures, such as King David and the prophet Elijah, experienced intense emotional highs and lows, which can resonate with the experiences of those living with bipolar disorder.

Psalm 38:6-8 captures a glimpse of David's emotional turmoil: "I am bowed down and brought very low; all day long I go about mourning. My back is filled with searing pain; there is no health in my body. I am feeble and utterly crushed; I groan in anguish of heart."

This passage reflects the deep emotional pain that can accompany mental health challenges, reminding us that such struggles are not foreign to the biblical narrative.

At the same time, it is important to recognize that bipolar disorder is a medical condition that requires appropriate treatment. Just as we seek medical care for physical illnesses, it is essential to pursue proper treatment for mental health conditions. Proverbs 19:20 advises, "Listen to advice and accept instruction, that you may gain wisdom in the future." Seeking medical advice and adhering to prescribed treatments are part of exercising wisdom in managing bipolar disorder.

Spiritual Practices for Managing Bipolar Disorder

Faith plays a crucial role in managing bipolar disorder, providing strength, comfort, and guidance. One of the foundational spiritual practices for individuals with bipolar disorder is prayer. Prayer allows you to bring your struggles before God, seek His wisdom, and experience His peace. Philippians 4:6-7 encourages believers, "Do not be anxious about anything, but in everything by prayer and supplication with thanksgiving let your requests be made known to God. And the peace of God, which surpasses all understanding, will guard your hearts and your minds in Christ Jesus." Regular prayer can help you stay grounded in your faith and maintain a sense of spiritual balance during mood fluctuations.

In addition to prayer, meditating on Scripture is vital for renewing your mind and finding stability in God's truth. Romans 12:2 instructs, "Do not be conformed to this world, but be transformed by the renewal of your mind, that by testing you may discern what is the will of God, what is good and acceptable and perfect." By immersing yourself in God's Word, you can counteract negative thought patterns and anchor your emotions in the unchanging truth of Scripture.

Worship is another powerful spiritual practice that can help manage the emotional swings associated with bipolar disorder. Whether through singing, listening to worship music, or reflecting on God's goodness, worship shifts your focus from your circumstances to God's greatness. Psalm 42:11 offers encouragement: "Why are you cast down, O my soul, and why are you in turmoil within me? Hope in God; for I shall again praise him, my salvation and my God." Worship helps to realign your perspective and cultivate a spirit of hope and gratitude.

It is also important to engage in regular fellowship with other believers. Hebrews 10:24-25 reminds us, "And let us consider how to stir up one another to love and good works, not neglecting to meet together, as is the habit of some, but encouraging one another, and all the more as you see the Day drawing near." Being part of a supportive Christian community provides encouragement, accountability, and a sense of belonging, which are essential for maintaining emotional and spiritual health.

Practical Steps to Actively Manage Bipolar Disorder

While spiritual practices are foundational, managing bipolar disorder also requires practical steps that address the physical and psychological aspects of the condition. One of the most important steps is to adhere to any prescribed treatment plan, which may include medication, therapy, and lifestyle changes. Proverbs 4:7 emphasizes the value of wisdom: "The beginning of wisdom is this: Get wisdom, and whatever you get, get insight." Following the guidance of healthcare professionals is a wise and necessary part of managing bipolar disorder.

Maintaining a regular routine is another key strategy. Bipolar disorder can disrupt sleep patterns, energy levels, and daily activities, so establishing a consistent schedule for sleep, meals, exercise, and other activities can help to stabilize mood. Ecclesiastes 3:1 states, "For everything there is a season, and a time for every matter under heaven." Creating a structured routine helps to bring order to your day and reduces the likelihood of mood swings triggered by irregular habits.

Monitoring your mood is an important aspect of managing bipolar disorder. Keeping a journal or using a mood-tracking app can help you identify patterns and triggers that affect your mood. Proverbs 27:23

advises, "Know well the condition of your flocks, and give attention to your herds." By staying aware of your emotional state, you can take proactive steps to address mood changes before they escalate.

Healthy lifestyle choices also play a significant role in managing bipolar disorder. Regular physical activity, a balanced diet, and sufficient sleep contribute to overall well-being and can help to regulate mood. 1 Corinthians 6:19-20 reminds us, "Or do you not know that your body is a temple of the Holy Spirit within you, whom you have from God? You are not your own, for you were bought with a price. So glorify God in your body." Taking care of your physical health is an important part of honoring God and supporting your mental health.

Stress management is another critical component. High levels of stress can trigger mood episodes, so it is important to develop strategies for managing stress. Techniques such as deep breathing, relaxation exercises, and engaging in enjoyable activities can help to reduce stress levels. Matthew 11:28-30 offers comfort: "Come to me, all who labor and are heavy laden, and I will give you rest. Take my yoke upon you, and learn from me, for I am gentle and lowly in heart, and you will find rest for your souls. For my yoke is easy, and my burden is light." Trusting in Jesus and finding rest in Him is the ultimate source of peace.

It is also essential to build a strong support system. Surrounding yourself with supportive family members, friends, and healthcare providers who understand your condition can provide encouragement, help you stay accountable to your treatment plan, and offer assistance during difficult times. Ecclesiastes 4:9-10 emphasizes the value of companionship: "Two are better than one, because they have a good reward for their toil. For if they fall, one will lift up his fellow. But woe to him who is alone when he falls and has not another to lift him up!" Having a network of supportive individuals is crucial for navigating the challenges of bipolar disorder.

Trusting in God's Sovereignty and Seeking His Strength

Living with bipolar disorder can be overwhelming, but it is important to remember that God is sovereign over all circumstances and that His strength is sufficient for every challenge. Psalm 46:1 declares, "God is our refuge and strength, a very present help in trouble." No matter how difficult your situation may be, you can trust that God is with you and that He will provide the strength you need to persevere.

One of the most comforting aspects of the Christian faith is the knowledge that God's grace is sufficient for every weakness. 2 Corinthians 12:9-10 records the apostle Paul's experience with a "thorn in the flesh," a persistent struggle that he asked God to remove. God's response was, "My grace is sufficient for you, for my power is made perfect in weakness." Paul then declares, "Therefore I will boast all the more gladly of my weaknesses, so that the power of Christ may rest upon me. For the sake of Christ, then, I am content with weaknesses, insults, hardships, persecutions, and calamities. For when I am weak, then I am strong." This passage reminds us that God's grace empowers us to endure our struggles and that His strength is made evident in our weaknesses.

In addition to relying on God's strength, it is important to cultivate hope in His promises. Living with bipolar disorder can sometimes feel discouraging, especially during difficult episodes, but the Bible offers hope that transcends circumstances. Romans 15:13 encourages believers, "May the God of hope fill you with all joy and peace in believing, so that by the power of the Holy Spirit you may abound in hope." By focusing on the hope that God provides, you can find joy and peace even in the midst of challenges.

Finally, it is important to remember that your identity is not defined by your diagnosis but by your relationship with Christ. 1 Peter 2:9-10 reminds us, "But you are a chosen race, a royal priesthood, a holy nation, a people for his own possession, that you may proclaim the excellencies of him who called you out of darkness into his marvelous light. Once you were not a people, but now you are God's people; once you had not received mercy, but now you have received mercy." Your worth and identity are rooted in who you are in Christ, not in your struggles.

Taking an active role in managing bipolar disorder involves integrating your faith with practical strategies that support your mental, emotional, and spiritual health. By relying on God's strength, adhering to your treatment plan, and engaging in spiritual practices, you can navigate the challenges of bipolar disorder and live a life that honors God.

CHAPTER 15 How Can You Gain Control Over Your Obsessive-Compulsive Disorder?

Obsessive-Compulsive Disorder (OCD) is a mental health condition characterized by intrusive, unwanted thoughts (obsessions) and repetitive behaviors or mental acts (compulsions) that individuals feel driven to perform in response to these thoughts. For those living with OCD, these patterns can be distressing and interfere with daily life. However, with a combination of biblical principles, cognitive-behavioral strategies, and practical steps, individuals can gain control over OCD and live a life aligned with God's peace and purpose.

Understanding OCD: A Biblical and Psychological Overview

OCD is a condition that affects the mind, leading to a cycle of obsessions and compulsions. These obsessions often involve fears, doubts, or concerns that are irrational or exaggerated, while the compulsions are behaviors intended to alleviate the anxiety caused by these thoughts. Although the Bible does not specifically mention OCD, it does address the struggle with anxious thoughts and the need for mental renewal.

Philippians 4:6-7 offers comfort and direction: "Do not be anxious about anything, but in everything by prayer and supplication with thanksgiving let your requests be made known to God. And the peace of God, which surpasses all understanding, will guard your hearts and your minds in Christ Jesus." This passage highlights the importance of bringing our concerns to God in prayer and trusting in

His peace, which transcends the fears and anxieties that often accompany OCD.

From a psychological perspective, OCD is understood as a disorder involving both cognitive distortions (irrational thoughts) and behavioral reinforcement (compulsive actions). The intrusive thoughts cause distress, and the compulsive behaviors are performed in an attempt to reduce this distress, creating a cycle that can be difficult to break. However, with the right tools, it is possible to challenge and change these patterns.

Spiritual Practices for Addressing OCD

For Christians dealing with OCD, spiritual practices are essential in managing the condition and finding peace. One of the most powerful tools in the Christian's arsenal is prayer. Prayer allows you to bring your obsessive thoughts and compulsive urges before God, seeking His help and strength to overcome them. Psalm 55:22 encourages us to "Cast your burden on Jehovah, and he will sustain you; he will never permit the righteous to be moved." This verse reminds us that God is our sustainer, and He is more than able to carry the burdens that weigh us down.

In addition to prayer, immersing yourself in Scripture is vital for renewing your mind and combating the distorted thinking patterns that characterize OCD. Romans 12:2 instructs, "Do not be conformed to this world, but be transformed by the renewal of your mind, that by testing you may discern what is the will of God, what is good and acceptable and perfect." By regularly reading, meditating on, and memorizing Scripture, you can fill your mind with God's truth, which counteracts the lies and fears that fuel OCD.

Worship is another powerful practice that can help manage OCD. Worshiping God, whether through singing, listening to worship music, or spending time in praise, shifts your focus from your obsessions to the greatness and goodness of God. Psalm 100:2-3 exhorts, "Serve Jehovah with gladness! Come into his presence with singing! Know that Jehovah, he is God! It is he who made us, and we are his; we are his people, and the sheep of his pasture." Worship helps to recalibrate your mind and heart, grounding you in the reality of God's sovereignty and care.

Engaging in fellowship with other believers is also crucial. The Christian life is not meant to be lived in isolation, and being part of a supportive community can provide encouragement, accountability, and prayer support. Hebrews 10:24-25 reminds us, "And let us consider how to stir up one another to love and good works, not neglecting to meet together, as is the habit of some, but encouraging one another, and all the more as you see the Day drawing near." Sharing your struggles with trusted friends, family members, or church leaders can help you feel less alone and provide practical support as you work to overcome OCD.

Cognitive-Behavioral Strategies for Managing OCD

While spiritual practices are foundational, cognitive-behavioral strategies are also effective in managing OCD. One of the key cognitive techniques is identifying and challenging the irrational thoughts that underlie your obsessions. These thoughts often involve catastrophic thinking, such as the belief that something terrible will happen if you do not perform a certain compulsion. 2 Corinthians 10:5 encourages us to "take every thought captive to obey Christ," which involves scrutinizing these thoughts and aligning them with biblical truth.

A practical way to challenge irrational thoughts is to ask yourself questions that help you assess their validity. For example, "Is this thought based on reality or fear?" or "What evidence do I have that supports or contradicts this belief?" By examining your thoughts critically, you can begin to see the distortions and replace them with more accurate and biblically grounded thinking.

Another cognitive-behavioral strategy is exposure and response prevention (ERP). ERP involves gradually exposing yourself to the triggers of your obsessions without engaging in the compulsive behaviors that you typically use to reduce anxiety. This process helps to break the cycle of OCD by allowing you to experience the anxiety and learn that it will decrease over time without the need for compulsions. Although ERP can be challenging, it is one of the most effective treatments for OCD when done under the guidance of a qualified therapist.

While engaging in ERP, it is essential to rely on God's strength and presence. Isaiah 41:10 provides reassurance: "Fear not, for I am with you; be not dismayed, for I am your God; I will strengthen you, I will help you, I will uphold you with my righteous right hand." Trusting in God's promise to be with you and sustain you can provide the courage needed to face your fears and resist the urge to perform compulsions.

In addition to ERP, practicing mindfulness can help manage OCD symptoms. Mindfulness involves focusing on the present moment and accepting your thoughts and feelings without judgment. Philippians 4:8 encourages believers to think about things that are true, honorable, just, pure, lovely, commendable, excellent, and praiseworthy. Mindfulness helps to cultivate this kind of thinking by keeping your mind focused on the here and now, rather than getting caught up in obsessive thoughts or compulsive behaviors.

Practical Steps to Support OCD Management

Alongside cognitive-behavioral strategies, there are practical steps you can take to support the management of OCD. One important step is to maintain a consistent daily routine. OCD can cause disruptions in daily life, but establishing and sticking to a routine can help provide structure and reduce the opportunities for obsessions and compulsions to take over. Ecclesiastes 3:1 reminds us, "For everything there is a season, and a time for every matter under heaven." Creating a routine that includes time for prayer, work, rest, and relaxation can help you stay balanced and focused.

Taking care of your physical health is also essential. Regular exercise, sufficient sleep, and a balanced diet contribute to overall well-being and can help reduce anxiety and stress, which often exacerbate OCD symptoms. 1 Corinthians 6:19-20 emphasizes the importance of caring for your body as a temple of the Holy Spirit. By prioritizing your physical health, you are also supporting your mental and emotional well-being.

It is also important to set realistic goals and expectations for yourself. Overcoming OCD is a process that takes time, and it is essential to be patient with yourself as you work toward progress. James 1:4 encourages perseverance: "And let steadfastness have its full effect, that you may be perfect and complete, lacking in nothing." Recognizing that healing and growth take time can help you stay committed to the journey, even when it feels difficult.

Building a support network is another crucial step. Surrounding yourself with people who understand your condition and can offer encouragement, accountability, and prayer support is invaluable. Ecclesiastes 4:9-10 highlights the importance of companionship: "Two are better than one, because they have a good reward for their toil. For if they fall, one will lift up his fellow." Having trusted friends, family members, or support groups can make a significant difference in your ability to manage OCD.

Finally, it is important to practice self-compassion. OCD can be a frustrating and exhausting condition, and it is easy to become critical of yourself when you struggle to manage your symptoms. However, Psalm 103:13-14 reminds us, "As a father shows compassion to his children, so Jehovah shows compassion to those who fear him. For he knows our frame; he remembers that we are dust." God understands your struggles and offers His compassion and grace. Extending that same compassion to yourself is an important part of the healing process.

Trusting in God's Faithfulness as You Manage OCD

Living with OCD can be challenging, but it is important to remember that God is faithful and present in every aspect of your life. Lamentations 3:22-23 declares, "The steadfast love of Jehovah never ceases; his mercies never come to an end; they are new every morning;

great is your faithfulness." This passage reassures us that God's love and mercy are constant, even in the midst of struggles with OCD.

Trusting in God's faithfulness involves surrendering your fears, doubts, and compulsions to Him, knowing that He is in control and that He is working all things for your good. Romans 8:28 encourages, "And we know that for those who love God all things work together for good, for those who are called according to his purpose." As you navigate the challenges of OCD, you can trust that God is with you and that He will use even your struggles for a greater purpose.

It is also important to remember that your identity is not defined by OCD but by your relationship with Christ. 2 Corinthians 5:17 affirms, "Therefore, if anyone is in Christ, he is a new creation. The old has passed away; behold, the new has come." Your worth and identity are rooted in who you are in Christ, not in the struggles you face.

In conclusion, gaining control over OCD requires a combination of spiritual practices, cognitive-behavioral strategies, and practical steps. By relying on God's strength, engaging in prayer and Scripture, and using the tools provided by cognitive-behavioral therapy, you can manage OCD and live a life that reflects God's peace and purpose.

CHAPTER 16 How Does the Bible Address Anxiety, and What Path to Freedom Does It Offer?

Anxiety is a common struggle that affects many individuals, manifesting as worry, fear, or unease about various aspects of life. While anxiety can range from mild to severe, it often leaves individuals feeling overwhelmed and helpless. The Bible acknowledges the reality of anxiety but also provides guidance on how to address it and offers a path to freedom through faith in God. This chapter will explore the biblical perspective on anxiety, the spiritual and practical steps to overcome it, and how to find lasting peace and freedom through a relationship with God.

Understanding Anxiety from a Biblical Perspective

Anxiety is an emotion that is often characterized by a sense of impending danger or concern about the future. In the Bible, anxiety is frequently mentioned in the context of worry or fear about life's uncertainties. Jesus Himself addressed the issue of anxiety in the Sermon on the Mount, where He encouraged His followers not to be anxious about their needs. In Matthew 6:25-27, Jesus says, "Therefore I tell you, do not be anxious about your life, what you will eat or what you will drink, nor about your body, what you will put on. Is not life more than food, and the body more than clothing? Look at the birds of the air: they neither sow nor reap nor gather into barns, and yet your heavenly Father feeds them. Are you not of more value than they? And which of you by being anxious can add a single hour to his span of life?"

In this passage, Jesus highlights the futility of anxiety and points to the trustworthiness of God, who cares for all His creation. The underlying message is clear: anxiety arises when we fail to trust in God's provision and sovereignty. By shifting our focus from our worries to God's faithfulness, we can begin to overcome anxiety.

The Bible also acknowledges that anxiety can be a response to specific threats or challenges. The psalmists, for example, often expressed their anxieties and fears to God in prayer. Psalm 94:19 states, "When the cares of my heart are many, your consolations cheer my soul." This verse reflects the reality that even those with strong faith can experience anxiety, but it also underscores the importance of turning to God for comfort and reassurance.

The Spiritual Path to Overcoming Anxiety

Overcoming anxiety begins with a spiritual foundation rooted in faith and trust in God. One of the most important spiritual practices for addressing anxiety is prayer. Prayer is the means by which you can bring your worries, fears, and concerns before God, seeking His peace and guidance. Philippians 4:6-7 offers clear instructions: "Do not be anxious about anything, but in everything by prayer and supplication with thanksgiving let your requests be made known to God. And the peace of God, which surpasses all understanding, will guard your hearts and your minds in Christ Jesus." This passage encourages believers to replace anxiety with prayer, trusting that God's peace will guard their hearts and minds.

In addition to prayer, meditating on Scripture is a powerful way to combat anxiety. God's Word is filled with promises of His presence, care, and provision, which can bring comfort and reassurance to a troubled heart. Isaiah 41:10 is a verse that offers such comfort: "Fear not, for I am with you; be not dismayed, for I am your God; I will strengthen you, I will help you, I will uphold you with my righteous right hand." By meditating on verses like this, you can remind yourself of God's faithfulness and find strength to face your anxieties.

Another important spiritual practice is worship. Worshiping God through song, praise, and thanksgiving shifts your focus from your problems to His greatness and power. Psalm 34:4 declares, "I sought Jehovah, and he answered me and delivered me from all my fears." Worship has the ability to lift your spirit and bring you into a place of peace and trust in God's sovereignty.

Fellowship with other believers is also crucial in dealing with anxiety. Being part of a supportive Christian community provides encouragement, prayer support, and accountability. Hebrews 10:24-25 emphasizes the importance of fellowship: "And let us consider how to stir up one another to love and good works, not neglecting to meet together, as is the habit of some, but encouraging one another, and all the more as you see the Day drawing near." Sharing your struggles with trusted friends or mentors can help alleviate the burden of anxiety and remind you that you are not alone in your journey.

Practical Steps to Overcoming Anxiety

While spiritual practices are essential, it is also important to take practical steps to address anxiety. One of the first steps is to identify the specific sources of your anxiety. By pinpointing what is causing your worry or fear, you can begin to address these issues more effectively. Proverbs 4:23 advises, "Keep your heart with all vigilance, for from it flow the springs of life." This verse highlights the importance of guarding your heart and mind against the influences that can lead to anxiety.

Once you have identified the sources of your anxiety, it is important to challenge the thoughts and beliefs that contribute to your anxious feelings. Anxiety often involves catastrophic thinking or a focus on worst-case scenarios. 2 Corinthians 10:5 encourages believers to "take every thought captive to obey Christ." By examining your thoughts and comparing them to the truth of God's Word, you can begin to replace anxious thoughts with thoughts that are rooted in faith and trust.

Another practical step is to practice mindfulness and relaxation techniques. These techniques can help you stay grounded in the present moment and reduce the physical symptoms of anxiety, such as rapid heart rate and shallow breathing. Psalm 46:10 offers a reminder to be still and trust in God: "Be still, and know that I am God. I will be exalted among the nations, I will be exalted in the earth!" Taking time to be still and focus on God's presence can help calm your mind and body.

In addition to mindfulness, it is important to maintain a healthy lifestyle that supports your mental and emotional well-being. Regular physical activity, a balanced diet, and sufficient sleep are all important factors in managing anxiety. 1 Corinthians 6:19-20 reminds us of the importance of caring for our bodies: "Or do you not know that your body is a temple of the Holy Spirit within you, whom you have from God? You are not your own, for you were bought with a price. So glorify God in your body." By taking care of your physical health, you are also supporting your mental and emotional health.

It is also helpful to set aside time each day for rest and relaxation. In a world that often glorifies busyness, it is important to prioritize rest and allow yourself time to recharge. Exodus 20:8-10 highlights the principle of rest: "Remember the Sabbath day, to keep it holy. Six days you shall labor, and do all your work, but the seventh day is a Sabbath to Jehovah your God." While the Sabbath is a specific day of rest, the principle of taking regular breaks and allowing time for rest is applicable to daily life.

Another practical step in overcoming anxiety is to seek professional help when needed. While spiritual practices and self-care are important, there may be times when additional support is necessary. Proverbs 15:22 states, "Without counsel plans fail, but with many advisers they succeed." Seeking counsel from a trusted Christian therapist or counselor can provide you with additional tools and strategies for managing anxiety.

The Path to Lasting Freedom from Anxiety

The ultimate path to freedom from anxiety lies in a deep and abiding trust in God. Trusting in God's sovereignty and His care for you is the foundation of overcoming anxiety. Proverbs 3:5-6 offers clear guidance: "Trust in Jehovah with all your heart, and do not lean on your own understanding. In all your ways acknowledge him, and he will make straight your paths." Trusting in God means surrendering your fears and worries to Him and believing that He is in control, even when circumstances are uncertain.

In addition to trust, cultivating a heart of gratitude can help you overcome anxiety. Gratitude shifts your focus from what is lacking or uncertain to the blessings that God has already provided. Philippians 4:6-7 encourages believers to combine prayer with thanksgiving: "Do not be anxious about anything, but in everything by prayer and supplication with thanksgiving let your requests be made known to God." Gratitude helps to counteract anxiety by reminding you of God's goodness and faithfulness.

It is also important to keep an eternal perspective. Anxiety often arises from a focus on temporary, earthly concerns. Colossians 3:2 encourages believers to "Set your minds on things that are above, not on things that are on earth." By keeping your focus on the eternal promises of God and the hope of heaven, you can find peace even in the midst of life's uncertainties.

Finally, remember that overcoming anxiety is a journey that requires patience and persistence. Psalm 27:14 offers encouragement: "Wait for Jehovah; be strong, and let your heart take courage; wait for Jehovah!" As you continue to seek God, trust in His promises, and apply the practical steps outlined in this chapter, you can experience the peace and freedom that God desires for you.

CHAPTER 17 How Can You Overcome Procrastination Through Biblical Principles and Practical Steps?

Procrastination is a common challenge that affects many individuals, often leading to stress, missed opportunities, and a sense of guilt or failure. It is the act of delaying or postponing tasks, despite knowing that doing so can have negative consequences. The Bible provides wisdom on the importance of diligence and stewardship of time, offering both spiritual guidance and practical steps to help overcome procrastination. This chapter will explore how to address procrastination by understanding its root causes, applying biblical principles, and implementing practical strategies to become more disciplined and effective in your daily life.

Understanding the Root Causes of Procrastination: A Biblical Insight

Procrastination is not merely a matter of poor time management; it often has deeper emotional and psychological roots. It can stem from fear of failure, perfectionism, a lack of motivation, or even a reluctance to face unpleasant tasks. The Bible acknowledges the human tendency to delay and warns against the dangers of procrastination. Proverbs 24:30-34 offers a vivid picture of the consequences of neglecting one's responsibilities: "I passed by the field of a sluggard, by the vineyard of a man lacking sense, and behold, it was all overgrown with thorns; the ground was covered with nettles, and its stone wall was broken down. Then I saw and considered it; I looked and received instruction. A little sleep, a little slumber, a little folding of the hands to rest, and poverty will come upon you like a robber, and want like an armed man."

This passage highlights the gradual but inevitable decline that occurs when we procrastinate. It also emphasizes the importance of diligence and the need to address tasks promptly. The "sluggard" is not necessarily lazy in the traditional sense but may be someone who procrastinates due to various reasons, resulting in the deterioration of what they are responsible for.

Procrastination can also be linked to a lack of trust in God's provision and timing. Sometimes, people delay action because they are uncertain about the future or are waiting for the "perfect" moment, which may never come. Ecclesiastes 11:4 warns, "He who observes the wind will not sow, and he who regards the clouds will not reap." This verse encourages taking action even when circumstances are not ideal, trusting that God will guide and provide as we step out in faith.

Biblical Principles for Overcoming Procrastination

To overcome procrastination, it is essential to apply biblical principles that address both the spiritual and practical aspects of this challenge. One of the foundational principles is the importance of stewardship. The Bible teaches that we are stewards of the time, talents, and resources that God has entrusted to us, and we are called to use them wisely. Ephesians 5:15-16 urges, "Look carefully then how you walk, not as unwise but as wise, making the best use of the time, because the days are evil." This passage reminds us that time is a precious resource, and we must be intentional about how we use it.

Another key principle is the call to diligence. Proverbs 10:4-5 states, "A slack hand causes poverty, but the hand of the diligent makes rich. He who gathers in summer is a prudent son, but he who sleeps in harvest is a son who brings shame." Diligence involves being proactive, disciplined, and consistent in our efforts, whether in work, ministry, or personal responsibilities. By cultivating a habit of diligence, we can overcome the tendency to procrastinate and ensure that we are fulfilling our God-given responsibilities.

The principle of seeking God's guidance and wisdom is also crucial in addressing procrastination. James 1:5 encourages believers,

"If any of you lacks wisdom, let him ask God, who gives generously to all without reproach, and it will be given him." When faced with tasks that seem overwhelming or unclear, it is important to seek God's wisdom and direction. Prayerfully asking for His guidance can provide the clarity and motivation needed to take the necessary steps forward.

Another biblical principle that can help combat procrastination is the practice of accountability. Ecclesiastes 4:9-10 highlights the value of having a partner or community to provide support and encouragement: "Two are better than one, because they have a good reward for their toil. For if they fall, one will lift up his fellow. But woe to him who is alone when he falls and has not another to lift him up!" Sharing your goals and challenges with a trusted friend, mentor, or accountability partner can help you stay on track and overcome the temptation to delay important tasks.

Practical Steps to Overcome Procrastination

While biblical principles provide the foundation, practical steps are necessary to implement these principles effectively in daily life. One of the most effective strategies is to break down large tasks into smaller, manageable steps. Proverbs 21:5 advises, "The plans of the diligent lead surely to abundance, but everyone who is hasty comes only to poverty." By planning carefully and breaking tasks into smaller parts, you can reduce the feeling of being overwhelmed and make steady progress.

Creating a daily or weekly schedule can also help you stay organized and focused. Setting specific times for tasks and sticking to a routine can prevent procrastination from taking hold. Psalm 90:12 offers a prayer for wisdom in using our time: "So teach us to number our days that we may get a heart of wisdom." Establishing a schedule that reflects your priorities and responsibilities is a practical way to "number your days" and use your time wisely.

Another practical step is to eliminate distractions that contribute to procrastination. In today's digital age, distractions such as social media, emails, and entertainment can easily derail your focus. Proverbs

4:25-27 advises, "Let your eyes look directly forward, and your gaze be straight before you. Ponder the path of your feet; then all your ways will be sure. Do not swerve to the right or to the left; turn your foot away from evil." This passage encourages maintaining focus and avoiding distractions that can lead you off course. By creating an environment that minimizes distractions, you can stay focused on your tasks and reduce the likelihood of procrastination.

Setting deadlines for yourself is another effective way to combat procrastination. Even if a task does not have an external deadline, setting an internal deadline can create a sense of urgency and motivation to complete the task. Colossians 3:23 reminds us, "Whatever you do, work heartily, as for Jehovah and not for men." By approaching tasks with the mindset of doing them for God, you can be motivated to complete them promptly and with excellence.

It is also important to address any underlying fears or anxieties that contribute to procrastination. Fear of failure, fear of making mistakes, or fear of the unknown can all lead to delays in taking action. Isaiah 41:10 provides reassurance: "Fear not, for I am with you; be not dismayed, for I am your God; I will strengthen you, I will help you, I will uphold you with my righteous right hand." Trusting in God's presence and strength can help you overcome these fears and move forward with confidence.

Finally, it is important to practice self-compassion and patience. Overcoming procrastination is a process that takes time, and there may be setbacks along the way. Philippians 1:6 offers encouragement: "And I am sure of this, that he who began a good work in you will bring it to completion at the day of Jesus Christ." By recognizing that growth and improvement take time, you can avoid becoming discouraged and continue to make progress.

Trusting in God's Faithfulness as You Overcome Procrastination

Overcoming procrastination requires both spiritual and practical efforts, but ultimately, it is about trusting in God's faithfulness and relying on His strength. Proverbs 3:5-6 encourages, "Trust in Jehovah with all your heart, and do not lean on your own understanding. In all your ways acknowledge him, and he will make straight your paths." Trusting in God involves surrendering your plans, fears, and tendencies to procrastinate to Him, knowing that He will guide and direct your steps.

In addition to trusting in God, it is important to cultivate a heart of gratitude and contentment. Procrastination can sometimes stem from a lack of contentment or dissatisfaction with the tasks at hand. Philippians 4:11-13 offers insight into finding contentment in every situation: "Not that I am speaking of being in need, for I have learned in whatever situation I am to be content. I know how to be brought low, and I know how to abound. In any and every circumstance, I have learned the secret of facing plenty and hunger, abundance and need. I can do all things through him who strengthens me." By focusing on the blessings and opportunities that God has provided, you can approach your tasks with a sense of purpose and gratitude.

Overcoming procrastination is not just about productivity; it is about living a life that reflects God's character and fulfills His purposes. By applying biblical principles, taking practical steps, and trusting in God's faithfulness, you can overcome procrastination and live a life of diligence, discipline, and devotion to God.

CHAPTER 18 Why Is Self-Control Essential for Christian Living and How Can It Be Cultivated?

Self-control is a fundamental aspect of Christian character and spiritual maturity. It is the ability to regulate one's emotions, thoughts, and behaviors in accordance with the will of God, resisting the impulses that lead to sin and choosing instead the path of righteousness. In a world that often glorifies indulgence and self-gratification, the importance of self-control cannot be overstated. This chapter will explore the biblical basis for self-control, the challenges to developing it, and practical steps for cultivating this vital fruit of the Spirit.

The Biblical Basis for Self-Control

The Bible frequently emphasizes the importance of self-control as a key aspect of living a life that honors God. Self-control is one of the fruits of the Spirit listed in Galatians 5:22-23: "But the fruit of the Spirit is love, joy, peace, patience, kindness, goodness, faithfulness, gentleness, self-control; against such things, there is no law." This passage highlights that self-control, like the other fruits, is a product of the Holy Spirit's work in the life of a believer. It is not something that we can achieve on our own but is cultivated through a close and obedient relationship with God.

The necessity of self-control is also underscored in Proverbs 25:28, which states, "A man without self-control is like a city broken into and left without walls." This vivid imagery depicts the vulnerability and chaos that result from a lack of self-control. Just as a city without walls is defenseless against invaders, a person without self-control is susceptible to the attacks of sin, temptation, and destructive behaviors.

Self-control acts as a protective barrier, guarding the heart and mind against the influences that would lead us away from God's will.

The apostle Paul also emphasized the importance of self-control in his letters. In 1 Corinthians 9:25-27, he writes, "Every athlete exercises self-control in all things. They do it to receive a perishable wreath, but we an imperishable. So I do not run aimlessly; I do not box as one beating the air. But I discipline my body and keep it under control, lest after preaching to others I myself should be disqualified." Here, Paul compares the Christian life to an athletic competition, where self-control is necessary for achieving the goal. Just as athletes exercise discipline and restraint to reach their goals, Christians must practice self-control to remain faithful and effective in their walk with God.

Moreover, self-control is essential for resisting the temptations that lead to sin. James 1:14-15 warns, "But each person is tempted when he is lured and enticed by his own desire. Then desire when it has conceived gives birth to sin, and sin when it is fully grown brings forth death." This passage highlights the progression from desire to sin and ultimately to death, illustrating the critical role that self-control plays in breaking this cycle. By exercising self-control, believers can resist the initial temptations and prevent the destructive consequences of sin.

Challenges to Developing Self-Control

While self-control is a vital aspect of Christian living, it is not always easy to develop or maintain. Several challenges can hinder the cultivation of self-control, including the influence of the flesh, societal pressures, and spiritual warfare.

One of the primary challenges to self-control is the ongoing struggle with the flesh—the sinful nature that resides in every person. Romans 7:18-19 describes this internal battle: "For I know that nothing good dwells in me, that is, in my flesh. For I have the desire to do what is right, but not the ability to carry it out. For I do not do the good I want, but the evil I do not want is what I keep on doing." This passage reflects the difficulty of consistently exercising self-control in the face of the flesh's desires. The flesh seeks immediate gratification and is often at odds with the Spirit's leading, making it a constant challenge to practice self-control.

Societal pressures also play a significant role in undermining self-control. We live in a culture that often promotes indulgence, self-centeredness, and the pursuit of pleasure without regard for the consequences. Messages from media, advertising, and even social norms can encourage individuals to "follow their hearts" or "do what feels right," often at the expense of self-discipline and obedience to God. Romans 12:2 warns against conforming to the world's patterns: "Do not be conformed to this world, but be transformed by the renewal of your mind, that by testing you may discern what is the will of God, what is good and acceptable and perfect." Overcoming these societal influences requires a deliberate effort to renew the mind with God's truth and to prioritize His will over worldly desires.

Spiritual warfare is another challenge to developing self-control. As Christians, we face an enemy who seeks to tempt, deceive, and destroy our faith. Ephesians 6:12 reminds us, "For we do not wrestle against flesh and blood, but against the rulers, against the authorities, against the cosmic powers over this present darkness, against the spiritual forces of evil in the heavenly places." Satan and his forces actively work to exploit our weaknesses and lead us into sin, making it essential to be vigilant and to rely on God's strength in the battle for self-control.

Cultivating Self-Control Through Spiritual Practices

Given the challenges to self-control, it is crucial to engage in spiritual practices that cultivate this fruit of the Spirit. One of the most effective ways to develop self-control is through regular prayer and dependence on God. Prayer is a means of inviting God's power and guidance into your life, acknowledging your need for His help in overcoming the desires of the flesh. Jesus Himself taught the importance of prayer in resisting temptation in Matthew 26:41: "Watch and pray that you may not enter into temptation. The spirit indeed is willing, but the flesh is weak." By maintaining a consistent prayer life, you can draw on God's strength to exercise self-control in moments of weakness.

Fasting is another spiritual discipline that can help cultivate self-control. Fasting involves voluntarily abstaining from food or other pleasures for a set period to focus on God and seek His will. Isaiah 58:6 describes the kind of fast that God desires: "Is not this the fast that I choose: to loose the bonds of wickedness, to undo the straps of the yoke, to let the oppressed go free, and to break every yoke?" Fasting teaches self-discipline by denying the flesh and prioritizing spiritual nourishment over physical desires. It is a powerful way to train the body and mind to submit to the Spirit's leading.

Studying and meditating on Scripture is also essential for developing self-control. God's Word provides guidance, encouragement, and correction, helping you align your thoughts and actions with His will. Psalm 119:9-11 emphasizes the role of Scripture in maintaining purity and self-control: "How can a young man keep his way pure? By guarding it according to your word. With my whole heart I seek you; let me not wander from your commandments! I have stored up your word in my heart, that I might not sin against you." By internalizing Scripture, you equip yourself with the truth needed to resist temptation and exercise self-control in all areas of life.

Fellowship with other believers is another important aspect of cultivating self-control. Hebrews 10:24-25 encourages Christians to support one another: "And let us consider how to stir up one another to love and good works, not neglecting to meet together, as is the habit of some, but encouraging one another, and all the more as you see the Day drawing near." Being part of a Christian community provides accountability, encouragement, and prayer support, all of which are vital for maintaining self-control. Sharing your struggles with trusted friends or mentors allows you to receive counsel, encouragement, and prayer, helping you stay on the path of righteousness.

Practical Strategies for Exercising Self-Control

In addition to spiritual practices, there are practical strategies that can help you exercise self-control in your daily life. One such strategy is setting clear and achievable goals. Proverbs 21:5 advises, "The plans of the diligent lead surely to abundance, but everyone who is hasty comes only to poverty." Setting specific goals and breaking them down into manageable steps can help you stay focused and disciplined. For example, if you struggle with overeating, setting a goal to eat smaller portions and planning your meals in advance can help you exercise self-control in this area.

Another practical strategy is to avoid situations that lead to temptation. Proverbs 4:14-15 offers wise counsel: "Do not enter the path of the wicked, and do not walk in the way of the evil. Avoid it; do not go on it; turn away from it and pass on." By identifying and avoiding situations that trigger sinful behavior, you can reduce the likelihood of falling into temptation. For instance, if you struggle with gossip, you might choose to avoid conversations or environments where gossip is prevalent.

Practicing mindfulness and self-awareness is also helpful in exercising self-control. Mindfulness involves being fully present in the moment and aware of your thoughts, feelings, and actions. 2 Corinthians 13:5 encourages self-examination: "Examine yourselves, to see whether you are in the faith. Test yourselves. Or do you not realize this about yourselves, that Jesus Christ is in you?—unless indeed you fail to meet the test!" By regularly examining your motives and behaviors, you can become more aware of areas where you need to exercise greater self-control and take corrective action.

Additionally, it is important to develop healthy habits that support self-control. For example, establishing a regular routine for prayer, Bible study, and physical exercise can help you maintain discipline and resist the urge to give in to impulsive behaviors. 1 Corinthians 9:27 reflects the importance of self-discipline: "But I discipline my body and keep it under control, lest after preaching to others I myself should be disqualified." Developing positive habits reinforces self-control and helps you stay committed to your goals.

Finally, practicing gratitude and contentment can help you cultivate self-control by shifting your focus from what you lack to what you have. Philippians 4:11-13 offers a powerful reminder of contentment: "Not that I am speaking of being in need, for I have learned in whatever situation I am to be content. I know how to be brought low, and I know how to abound. In any and every circumstance, I have learned the secret of facing plenty and hunger, abundance and need. I can do all things through him who strengthens me." By cultivating a heart of gratitude, you can reduce the desire for immediate gratification and remain focused on your long-term spiritual growth.

The Role of Prayer in Cultivating Self-Control

Prayer is central to the development of self-control because it aligns your will with God's will and invites His power into your life. As you seek to grow in self-control, it is important to pray specifically for this fruit of the Spirit to be evident in your life. Galatians 5:16 encourages, "But I say, walk by the Spirit, and you will not gratify the desires of the flesh." Prayer is a way to walk by the Spirit, asking God to help you resist the flesh and live according to His purposes.

In addition to praying for self-control, it is important to pray for strength and perseverance in the face of challenges. Jesus taught His disciples to pray for deliverance from temptation in Matthew 6:13: "And lead us not into temptation, but deliver us from evil." By consistently bringing your struggles to God in prayer, you can receive the strength and guidance needed to exercise self-control in difficult situations.

Finally, prayer should be paired with practical steps to work on behalf of your prayers. As you pray for self-control, consider what specific actions you can take to support your prayer. For example, if you are praying for self-control in managing your time, you might create a daily schedule or set boundaries on how much time you spend on certain activities. James 2:26 reminds us, "For as the body apart from the spirit is dead, so also faith apart from works is dead." True faith is active and involves taking steps to align your actions with your prayers.

Trusting in God's Power to Develop Self-Control

Developing self-control is a lifelong journey that requires both spiritual and practical efforts. It is important to remember that self-control is ultimately a work of the Holy Spirit in your life. Philippians 2:12-13 encourages believers, "Therefore, my beloved, as you have always obeyed, so now, not only as in my presence but much more in my absence, work out your own salvation with fear and trembling, for it is God who works in you, both to will and to work for his good pleasure." While you are called to actively pursue self-control, it is God who empowers you to do so.

In moments of weakness or failure, it is essential to rely on God's grace and forgiveness. 1 John 1:9 offers assurance: "If we confess our sins, he is faithful and just to forgive us our sins and to cleanse us from all unrighteousness." Rather than becoming discouraged by setbacks, you can trust in God's forgiveness and continue to pursue self-control with renewed determination.

By applying the biblical principles and practical strategies outlined in this chapter, you can cultivate self-control and live a life that reflects the character of Christ. As you grow in self-control, you will experience greater freedom from the impulses that lead to sin and greater alignment with God's will for your life.

CHAPTER 19 How Can You Overcome Alcoholism Through Biblical Wisdom and Practical Strategies?

Alcoholism is a pervasive issue that affects individuals, families, and communities, leading to physical, emotional, and spiritual harm. For those struggling with alcohol dependence, the journey to recovery can be daunting, but the Bible offers profound wisdom and hope for overcoming this challenge. This chapter will explore the biblical perspective on alcohol, the spiritual and practical steps necessary to overcome alcoholism, and how to maintain a life of sobriety through faith and reliance on God.

Understanding Alcoholism from a Biblical Perspective

The Bible acknowledges the use of alcohol but also provides clear warnings about its potential for misuse and the dangers of overindulgence. Wine was a common beverage in biblical times, and it is mentioned frequently in both the Old and New Testaments. However, the Bible also cautions against the excessive consumption of alcohol, recognizing its potential to lead individuals into sin and destruction.

Proverbs 20:1 states, "Wine is a mocker, strong drink a brawler, and whoever is led astray by it is not wise." This verse highlights the deceptive nature of alcohol—it may seem harmless or even enjoyable at first, but it can quickly lead to behaviors that are damaging to oneself and others. The term "led astray" implies a gradual process, where initial moderate drinking can evolve into dependency and addiction, leading to a loss of self-control and wisdom.

The New Testament also addresses the issue of drunkenness. Ephesians 5:18 commands, "And do not get drunk with wine, for that is debauchery, but be filled with the Spirit." Here, the apostle Paul contrasts being filled with alcohol, which leads to reckless behavior, with being filled with the Holy Spirit, which leads to righteous living. The underlying message is clear: reliance on alcohol is incompatible with a life that is surrendered to God and guided by His Spirit.

Additionally, the Bible emphasizes the importance of sobriety and self-control, which are essential for a life that honors God. 1 Peter 5:8 warns, "Be sober-minded; be watchful. Your adversary the devil prowls around like a roaring lion, seeking someone to devour." Sobriety is not just about abstaining from alcohol; it is about maintaining a clear and focused mind that is vigilant against the enemy's attacks. Alcoholism dulls the mind and weakens spiritual defenses, making individuals more vulnerable to temptation and sin.

The Spiritual Path to Overcoming Alcoholism

Overcoming alcoholism begins with acknowledging the problem and turning to God for help. This requires humility and a recognition of one's inability to overcome the addiction on their own. James 4:6-7 offers encouragement: "But he gives more grace. Therefore it says, 'God opposes the proud but gives grace to the humble.' Submit yourselves therefore to God. Resist the devil, and he will flee from you." The first step in overcoming alcoholism is to submit to God, admitting your need for His grace and strength to break free from the bondage of addiction.

Prayer is a crucial aspect of the recovery process. Through prayer, you can bring your struggles before God, seeking His guidance, strength, and healing. Philippians 4:6-7 provides comfort: "Do not be anxious about anything, but in everything by prayer and supplication with thanksgiving let your requests be made known to God. And the peace of God, which surpasses all understanding, will guard your hearts and your minds in Christ Jesus." Prayer not only brings your concerns to God but also invites His peace to guard your mind against the anxieties and triggers that often lead to drinking.

Another essential spiritual practice is repentance. Repentance involves turning away from sin and making a deliberate decision to change one's behavior. Acts 3:19 urges, "Repent therefore, and turn again, that your sins may be blotted out, that times of refreshing may come from the presence of Jehovah." Repentance is not just about feeling sorry for past mistakes; it is about making a commitment to live differently moving forward. For someone struggling with alcoholism, this may involve taking concrete steps to avoid situations that lead to drinking, seeking accountability, and replacing harmful habits with healthy ones.

Fasting can also be a powerful tool in the battle against alcoholism. Fasting involves abstaining from food or other pleasures to focus on God and seek His will. Isaiah 58:6 speaks of the kind of fast that pleases God: "Is not this the fast that I choose: to loose the bonds of wickedness, to undo the straps of the yoke, to let the oppressed go free, and to break every yoke?" Fasting can help break the physical and spiritual bonds of addiction by denying the flesh and relying on God for strength and sustenance.

Fellowship with other believers is another critical aspect of the spiritual path to overcoming alcoholism. Hebrews 10:24-25 emphasizes the importance of community: "And let us consider how to stir up one another to love and good works, not neglecting to meet together, as is the habit of some, but encouraging one another, and all the more as you see the Day drawing near." Being part of a supportive Christian community provides encouragement, prayer support, and accountability, all of which are vital for maintaining sobriety. Sharing your struggles with trusted friends or mentors allows you to receive counsel, encouragement, and prayer, helping you stay on the path of recovery.

Practical Strategies for Overcoming Alcoholism

In addition to the spiritual practices outlined above, practical strategies are necessary for overcoming alcoholism and maintaining sobriety. One of the most important strategies is to remove alcohol from your environment. Proverbs 4:14-15 advises, "Do not enter the path of the wicked, and do not walk in the way of evil. Avoid it; do not go on it; turn away from it and pass on." Removing alcohol from your home and avoiding places where you are likely to be tempted can help you resist the urge to drink.

Another practical strategy is to develop new habits and routines that support sobriety. 1 Corinthians 9:27 reflects the importance of discipline: "But I discipline my body and keep it under control, lest after preaching to others I myself should be disqualified." Establishing a daily routine that includes time for prayer, Bible study, exercise, and healthy activities can help you stay focused and avoid the triggers that lead to drinking.

It is also important to seek professional help when needed. Proverbs 15:22 states, "Without counsel plans fail, but with many advisers they succeed." Christian counseling, therapy, and support groups such as Alcoholics Anonymous can provide valuable tools and support for overcoming alcoholism. These resources can offer coping strategies, accountability, and encouragement to help you stay on the path of recovery.

Setting goals and celebrating milestones can also be motivating in the recovery process. Proverbs 13:12 highlights the power of hope: "Hope deferred makes the heart sick, but a desire fulfilled is a tree of life." Setting small, achievable goals can help you build confidence and see progress in your journey to sobriety. Whether it is a day, a week, or a month of sobriety, celebrating these milestones with gratitude to God can reinforce your commitment to staying sober.

Mindfulness and stress management techniques are also helpful in preventing relapse. Psalm 46:10 encourages, "Be still, and know that I am God." Practicing mindfulness—being present in the moment and aware of your thoughts and feelings—can help you manage stress and anxiety, which are common triggers for drinking. Techniques such as deep breathing, meditation, and relaxation exercises can help you stay calm and centered, reducing the urge to turn to alcohol for relief.

Finally, accountability is crucial in overcoming alcoholism. James 5:16 advises, "Therefore, confess your sins to one another and pray for one another, that you may be healed. The prayer of a righteous person has great power as it is working." Having an accountability partner or support group can provide the encouragement and accountability you need to stay on track. Regular check-ins with someone who understands your struggles can help you stay committed to your sobriety goals.

Maintaining a Life of Sobriety Through Faith and Action

Overcoming alcoholism is not just about quitting drinking; it is about maintaining a life of sobriety and living in accordance with God's will. This requires ongoing faith, discipline, and reliance on God's strength. Philippians 4:13 offers encouragement: "I can do all things through him who strengthens me." Trusting in God's power to sustain you is essential in maintaining long-term sobriety.

It is also important to continue growing in your faith and relationship with God. John 15:5 reminds us of the need to remain connected to Christ: "I am the vine; you are the branches. Whoever abides in me and I in him, he it is that bears much fruit, for apart from me you can do nothing." Regular prayer, Bible study, and fellowship with other believers are vital for staying spiritually strong and resisting the temptations that can lead to relapse.

In addition, practicing gratitude and contentment can help you maintain sobriety by shifting your focus from what you have given up to what you have gained. 1 Thessalonians 5:18 encourages, "Give thanks in all circumstances; for this is the will of God in Christ Jesus for you." By cultivating a heart of gratitude, you can remain focused on the blessings of sobriety and the new life that God has given you.

Serving others is another way to maintain sobriety and grow in your faith. Galatians 5:13 exhorts, "For you were called to freedom, brothers. Only do not use your freedom as an opportunity for the flesh, but through love serve one another." Serving others shifts your focus from your own struggles to the needs of others, providing a sense of purpose and fulfillment that can help you stay sober.

Finally, it is important to be patient with yourself and trust in God's timing. Overcoming alcoholism is a journey that takes time, and there may be setbacks along the way. Romans 8:28 offers reassurance: "And we know that for those who love God all things work together for good, for those who are called according to his purpose." Even in moments of struggle, trust that God is working in your life and that He will bring good out of every situation.

By applying these biblical principles and practical strategies, you can overcome alcoholism and live a life of sobriety that honors God. Remember that you are not alone in this journey—God is with you, and He will provide the strength and guidance you need to stay on the path of recovery.

CHAPTER 20 How Can Biblical Principles and Practical Strategies Help in Overcoming Eating Disorders?

Eating disorders, such as anorexia nervosa, bulimia nervosa, and binge-eating disorder, are complex and often life-threatening conditions that affect the physical, emotional, and spiritual well-being of individuals. These disorders are not merely about food or body image; they are rooted in deeper issues of identity, self-worth, and control. The Bible offers profound wisdom for addressing these underlying issues and provides a foundation for healing and recovery. This chapter will explore how biblical principles, combined with practical strategies, can help individuals overcome eating disorders and find freedom in Christ.

Understanding Eating Disorders from a Biblical Perspective

Eating disorders are a manifestation of deeper spiritual and emotional struggles. At their core, these disorders often involve a distorted self-image, a lack of self-worth, and a desire for control. The Bible addresses these issues by affirming the inherent value of every person, created in the image of God, and by offering hope and healing through a relationship with Jesus Christ.

Genesis 1:27 states, "So God created man in his own image, in the image of God he created him; male and female he created them." This verse affirms that every person is made in the image of God, with inherent dignity and worth. However, those struggling with eating disorders often struggle to see themselves as valuable or worthy of love. This distorted self-image can lead to behaviors aimed at achieving an unattainable standard of perfection, whether through extreme dieting, purging, or binge-eating.

The Bible also speaks to the issue of control, which is a significant factor in eating disorders. Proverbs 3:5-6 advises, "Trust in Jehovah with all your heart, and do not lean on your own understanding. In all your ways acknowledge him, and he will make straight your paths." Eating disorders often develop as a way to exert control over one's life in the face of uncertainty or emotional pain. However, true control comes from surrendering to God and trusting Him to guide and sustain us.

Moreover, the Bible addresses the issue of idolatry, which can be a factor in eating disorders. When individuals place an unhealthy focus on their appearance, body weight, or food, these things can become idols, taking the place of God in their lives. Exodus 20:3 warns, "You shall have no other gods before me." Overcoming an eating disorder requires recognizing and repenting of this idolatry, turning instead to God as the source of true identity and fulfillment.

The Spiritual Path to Healing and Recovery

Healing from an eating disorder begins with recognizing the spiritual roots of the disorder and turning to God for help. This process involves several key steps: repentance, renewal of the mind, reliance on God's strength, and embracing a new identity in Christ.

Repentance is the first step in the healing process. Repentance involves acknowledging the ways in which one's thoughts and behaviors have strayed from God's truth and making a deliberate decision to turn back to Him. Acts 3:19 encourages, "Repent therefore, and turn again, that your sins may be blotted out, that times of refreshing may come from the presence of Jehovah." Repentance is not just about feeling sorry for past mistakes; it is about making a commitment to live differently moving forward. This may involve confessing the sin of idolatry, surrendering the desire for control, and asking God to renew your mind and heart.

Renewal of the mind is essential for overcoming the distorted thinking that fuels eating disorders. Romans 12:2 instructs, "Do not be conformed to this world, but be transformed by the renewal of your mind, that by testing you may discern what is the will of God, what is good and acceptable and perfect." Renewing the mind involves replacing lies with God's truth—such as the belief that your worth is determined by your appearance or weight—with the truth that your worth is determined by God's love for you. This process requires regular meditation on Scripture, prayer, and the rejection of worldly standards of beauty and success.

Relying on God's strength is also crucial in the recovery process. Philippians 4:13 reminds us, "I can do all things through him who strengthens me." Overcoming an eating disorder is not something that can be done in one's own strength; it requires the power of God working in and through you. Prayer is a key component of relying on God's strength. Through prayer, you can bring your struggles before God, ask for His help, and receive the peace and strength needed to resist the temptations that lead to disordered eating behaviors.

Embracing a new identity in Christ is another vital aspect of recovery. 2 Corinthians 5:17 declares, "Therefore, if anyone is in Christ, he is a new creation. The old has passed away; behold, the new has come." In Christ, you are no longer defined by your past mistakes or your struggles with an eating disorder. Instead, you are a new creation, defined by your relationship with Christ and the love and acceptance that He offers. Embracing this new identity involves letting go of the lies that have held you captive and living out the truth of who you are in Christ.

Practical Strategies for Overcoming Eating Disorders

In addition to spiritual practices, there are practical strategies that can help you overcome an eating disorder and maintain a healthy relationship with food and your body. These strategies include seeking professional help, developing healthy eating habits, practicing mindfulness, and building a supportive community.

Seeking professional help is often a necessary step in the recovery process. Proverbs 11:14 states, "Where there is no guidance, a people falls, but in an abundance of counselors there is safety." Christian counseling, therapy, and support groups can provide valuable tools and support for overcoming an eating disorder. These resources can offer coping strategies, accountability, and encouragement to help you stay on the path of recovery. A therapist or counselor can help you identify and address the underlying issues that contribute to your eating disorder, such as trauma, anxiety, or low self-esteem.

Developing healthy eating habits is another important strategy for overcoming an eating disorder. 1 Corinthians 10:31 advises, "So, whether you eat or drink, or whatever you do, do all to the glory of God." Developing a healthy relationship with food involves recognizing that food is a gift from God, meant to nourish and sustain your body. It also involves learning to listen to your body's hunger and fullness cues, practicing moderation, and avoiding the extremes of restriction or bingeing. Working with a registered dietitian or nutritionist can be helpful in developing a balanced and healthy eating plan.

Practicing mindfulness can also aid in the recovery process. Mindfulness involves being fully present in the moment and aware of your thoughts, feelings, and actions. Philippians 4:8 encourages us to focus on what is true, honorable, just, pure, lovely, and commendable. Practicing mindfulness in relation to eating can help you become more aware of your body's needs, recognize triggers for disordered eating, and develop a healthier relationship with food. Techniques such as deep breathing, meditation, and mindful eating can help you stay calm and centered, reducing the urge to engage in disordered eating behaviors.

Building a supportive community is another key strategy for overcoming an eating disorder. Hebrews 10:24-25 emphasizes the importance of community: "And let us consider how to stir up one another to love and good works, not neglecting to meet together, as is the habit of some, but encouraging one another, and all the more as you see the Day drawing near." Being part of a supportive Christian community provides encouragement, prayer support, and accountability, all of which are vital for maintaining recovery. Sharing your struggles with trusted friends or mentors allows you to receive counsel, encouragement, and prayer, helping you stay on the path of healing.

The Role of Prayer in Overcoming Eating Disorders

Prayer is central to the recovery process because it aligns your will with God's will and invites His power into your life. As you seek to overcome an eating disorder, it is important to pray specifically for healing, strength, and a renewed mind. James 5:16 encourages, "Therefore, confess your sins to one another and pray for one another, that you may be healed. The prayer of a righteous person has great power as it is working." Prayer is not just a passive act; it is an active step of faith that brings your struggles before God and asks for His intervention.

In addition to praying for healing, it is important to pray for wisdom and discernment in the recovery process. Proverbs 3:5-6 advises, "Trust in Jehovah with all your heart, and do not lean on your own understanding. In all your ways acknowledge him, and he will make straight your paths." By seeking God's wisdom, you can make decisions that align with His will and lead to true healing and freedom.

Prayer should also be paired with practical steps to work on behalf of your prayers. For example, if you are praying for healing from an eating disorder, you might take steps such as seeking professional help, developing healthy eating habits, and building a supportive community. James 2:17 reminds us, "So also faith by itself, if it does not have works, is dead." True faith is active and involves taking steps to align your actions with your prayers.

Trusting in God's Power for Long-Term Recovery

Overcoming an eating disorder is not a one-time event; it is a lifelong journey that requires ongoing faith, discipline, and reliance on

God's strength. Philippians 1:6 offers encouragement: "And I am sure of this, that he who began a good work in you will bring it to completion at the day of Jesus Christ." Trusting in God's power to sustain you is essential in maintaining long-term recovery.

It is also important to continue growing in your faith and relationship with God. Colossians 2:6-7 encourages, "Therefore, as you received Christ Jesus the Lord, so walk in him, rooted and built up in him and established in the faith, just as you were taught, abounding in thanksgiving." Regular prayer, Bible study, and fellowship with other believers are vital for staying spiritually strong and resisting the temptations that can lead to relapse.

In moments of weakness or failure, it is essential to rely on God's grace and forgiveness. 1 John 1:9 offers assurance: "If we confess our sins, he is faithful and just to forgive us our sins and to cleanse us from all unrighteousness." Rather than becoming discouraged by setbacks, you can trust in God's forgiveness and continue to pursue healing and recovery with renewed determination.

By applying these biblical principles and practical strategies, you can overcome an eating disorder and live a life that honors God. Remember that you are not alone in this journey—God is with you, and He will provide the strength and guidance you need to stay on the path of recovery.

CHAPTER 21 How Can You Escape the Pornography Trap Through Biblical Counsel and Practical Steps?

The allure of pornography is a pervasive issue that entraps many individuals, leading to spiritual, emotional, and relational damage. As a sin that thrives in secrecy and shame, pornography can create a powerful stronghold in the life of a believer, hindering spiritual growth and damaging one's relationship with Jehovah. This chapter will explore the biblical perspective on sexual purity, the spiritual and practical steps necessary to escape the pornography trap, and how to maintain purity through a life surrendered to God.

Understanding Pornography from a Biblical Perspective

Pornography is fundamentally a distortion of God's design for human sexuality. The Bible teaches that sex is a gift from God, intended to be enjoyed within the confines of marriage between one man and one woman. Genesis 2:24 states, "Therefore a man shall leave his father and his mother and hold fast to his wife, and they shall become one flesh." This verse underscores the sacredness of the marital union, where sexual intimacy is an expression of love, commitment, and unity.

However, pornography corrupts this gift by reducing sex to a mere commodity, stripping it of its sacredness and reducing individuals to objects for selfish gratification. Jesus warned about the dangers of lust in Matthew 5:28: "But I say to you that everyone who looks at a woman with lustful intent has already committed adultery with her in his heart." This teaching highlights that sin begins in the heart and mind, not just in physical actions. Pornography fosters lustful thoughts, leading individuals to sin against God and others.

The Bible also emphasizes the importance of purity and holiness, especially in the area of sexual conduct. 1 Thessalonians 4:3-5 instructs, "For this is the will of God, your sanctification: that you abstain from sexual immorality; that each one of you know how to control his own body in holiness and honor, not in the passion of lust like the Gentiles who do not know God." This passage clearly calls believers to live lives that are set apart, marked by self-control and honor in their sexual behavior. Pornography, which fuels sexual immorality and lust, is in direct opposition to this call to holiness.

Moreover, pornography creates a barrier between the individual and God, as it is a sin that thrives in darkness and secrecy. Ephesians 5:11-12 warns, "Take no part in the unfruitful works of darkness, but instead expose them. For it is shameful even to speak of the things that they do in secret." The secretive nature of pornography leads to a cycle of shame and guilt, which can drive individuals further into isolation and away from the fellowship of believers and the presence of God.

The Spiritual Path to Freedom from Pornography

Breaking free from the pornography trap begins with a deep commitment to purity and a wholehearted pursuit of God. This journey requires repentance, renewal of the mind, reliance on God's strength, and active participation in spiritual disciplines.

Repentance is the first crucial step toward freedom. Repentance involves acknowledging the sin of engaging in pornography, confessing it to God, and turning away from it with a sincere heart. 1 John 1:9 offers a powerful promise: "If we confess our sins, he is faithful and just to forgive us our sins and to cleanse us from all unrighteousness." Confession and repentance are necessary for receiving God's forgiveness and cleansing, setting the stage for a new beginning.

Renewal of the mind is essential for overcoming the mental strongholds that pornography creates. Romans 12:2 instructs, "Do not be conformed to this world, but be transformed by the renewal of your mind, that by testing you may discern what is the will of God, what is good and acceptable and perfect." Renewing the mind involves replacing the lies and distortions of pornography with the truth of God's Word. Regular meditation on Scripture, prayer, and the rejection of worldly influences are key to transforming one's thought life and aligning it with God's will.

Relying on God's strength is also critical in the battle against pornography. Philippians 4:13 reminds us, "I can do all things through him who strengthens me." Overcoming the pull of pornography requires divine strength, as the flesh is weak and prone to temptation. Prayer is a powerful tool in this struggle, allowing individuals to seek God's help, guidance, and strength to resist temptation. Jesus taught His disciples to pray for deliverance from temptation in Matthew 6:13: "And lead us not into temptation, but deliver us from evil." Consistent, fervent prayer is essential for gaining victory over the stronghold of pornography.

Active participation in spiritual disciplines, such as prayer, fasting, and Bible study, is necessary for maintaining purity and staying close to God. Galatians 5:16 encourages, "But I say, walk by the Spirit, and you will not gratify the desires of the flesh." Walking by the Spirit involves daily surrender to God, allowing the Holy Spirit to guide and empower you to live in obedience to His Word. This spiritual discipline helps to cultivate a heart that desires holiness and purity, reducing the appeal of sinful behaviors such as pornography.

Practical Steps to Overcoming the Pornography Trap

In addition to spiritual practices, there are practical steps that can help you break free from the grip of pornography and maintain a life of purity. These steps include setting boundaries, seeking accountability, developing healthy habits, and addressing underlying issues.

Setting boundaries is a crucial step in overcoming pornography. Proverbs 4:23 advises, "Keep your heart with all vigilance, for from it flow the springs of life." Protecting your heart and mind from temptation requires setting clear boundaries regarding what you allow yourself to see and engage with. This may involve installing internet filters, avoiding websites or social media platforms that promote inappropriate content, and being mindful of the movies, shows, and books you consume. Creating a safe environment that minimizes exposure to pornography is essential for maintaining purity.

Seeking accountability is another important step in overcoming pornography. James 5:16 emphasizes the power of accountability: "Therefore, confess your sins to one another and pray for one another, that you may be healed. The prayer of a righteous person has great power as it is working." Having an accountability partner or joining a support group can provide the encouragement, support, and accountability needed to resist temptation and stay on the path of purity. Regular check-ins with someone who understands your struggles can help you stay committed to your goals and provide a safe space for confession and prayer.

Developing healthy habits is also essential in overcoming pornography. 1 Corinthians 9:27 reflects the importance of discipline: "But I discipline my body and keep it under control, lest after preaching to others I myself should be disqualified." Establishing a routine that includes regular exercise, healthy eating, sufficient rest, and engaging in fulfilling activities can help you reduce stress and avoid the triggers that lead to pornography use. Filling your life with positive, edifying activities can help you break free from the cycle of temptation and sin.

Addressing underlying issues is another key step in overcoming pornography. Often, pornography is a coping mechanism for deeper emotional or psychological issues, such as loneliness, stress, depression, or unresolved trauma. Proverbs 20:5 states, "The purpose in a man's heart is like deep water, but a man of understanding will draw it out." Seeking professional counseling or therapy can help you identify and address these underlying issues, providing tools and strategies for healthier ways of coping and healing.

The Role of Prayer and Scripture in Maintaining Purity

Prayer and Scripture are powerful tools in the battle against pornography, providing strength, guidance, and encouragement to maintain purity. As you seek to overcome pornography, it is important to incorporate both prayer and Scripture into your daily life.

Prayer is central to maintaining purity because it aligns your heart with God's will and invites His power into your life. As you pray, be specific in asking for God's help to resist temptation, to renew your mind, and to live in purity. Psalm 51:10 is a prayer for purity: "Create in me a clean heart, O God, and renew a right spirit within me." Praying for a clean heart and a right spirit is essential in overcoming the pull of pornography and staying close to God.

In addition to praying for purity, it is important to pray for strength and perseverance. Ephesians 6:10-11 encourages, "Finally, be strong in the Lord and in the strength of his might. Put on the whole armor of God, that you may be able to stand against the schemes of the devil." Prayer is a way to put on the armor of God, asking for His protection and strength to stand firm against the enemy's attacks.

Scripture is another powerful weapon in the battle against pornography. Hebrews 4:12 describes the power of God's Word: "For the word of God is living and active, sharper than any two-edged sword, piercing to the division of soul and of spirit, of joints and of marrow, and discerning the thoughts and intentions of the heart." Regularly reading, studying, and meditating on Scripture helps to renew your mind, strengthen your spirit, and resist the lies and temptations of pornography.

Memorizing Scripture is also helpful in the fight against pornography. When tempted, recalling specific verses can help you refocus your mind on God's truth and resist the urge to sin. Psalm 119:11 states, "I have stored up your word in my heart, that I might not sin against you." Storing God's Word in your heart equips you with the truth needed to combat the lies and temptations of pornography.

Finally, prayer and Scripture should be paired with practical steps to work on behalf of your prayers. James 2:26 reminds us, "For as the body apart from the spirit is dead, so also faith apart from works is dead." True faith is active and involves taking steps to align your actions with your prayers. If you are praying for freedom from pornography, take practical steps such as setting boundaries, seeking accountability, and developing healthy habits to support your spiritual growth and recovery.

Trusting in God's Power for Long-Term Victory

Overcoming pornography is not a one-time event but a lifelong journey that requires ongoing faith, discipline, and reliance on God's strength. Philippians 1:6 offers encouragement: "And I am sure of this, that he who began a good work in you will bring it to completion at the day of Jesus Christ." Trusting in God's power to sustain you is essential in maintaining long-term victory over pornography.

It is also important to continue growing in your faith and relationship with God. Colossians 2:6-7 encourages, "Therefore, as you received Christ Jesus the Lord, so walk in him, rooted and built up in him and established in the faith, just as you were taught, abounding in thanksgiving." Regular prayer, Bible study, and fellowship with other believers are vital for staying spiritually strong and resisting the temptations that can lead to relapse.

In moments of weakness or failure, it is essential to rely on God's grace and forgiveness. 1 John 1:9 offers assurance: "If we confess our sins, he is faithful and just to forgive us our sins and to cleanse us from all unrighteousness." Rather than becoming discouraged by setbacks, you can trust in God's forgiveness and continue to pursue purity with renewed determination.

By applying these biblical principles and practical strategies, you can break free from the pornography trap and live a life that honors God. Remember that you are not alone in this journey—God is with you, and He will provide the strength and guidance you need to stay on the path of purity.

CHAPTER 22 How Can You Overcome the Self-Abuse of Masturbation Through Biblical Counsel and Practical Action?

Masturbation is a topic that is often shrouded in secrecy and shame, yet it is a behavior that many struggle with privately. The Bible, while not directly addressing masturbation, provides principles that guide Christians in understanding the implications of this act and how it can be a form of self-abuse that undermines spiritual growth, emotional health, and relational integrity. This chapter will explore the biblical perspective on sexual purity, the spiritual and practical steps necessary to overcome the habit of masturbation, and how to maintain purity through a life surrendered to God.

Understanding Masturbation from a Biblical Perspective

Masturbation, while not explicitly mentioned in Scripture, can be understood within the broader biblical teachings on sexual purity, self-control, and the sanctity of the body. The Bible calls believers to a high standard of purity in both thought and action. Jesus' teaching in Matthew 5:28 is particularly relevant: "But I say to you that everyone who looks at a woman with lustful intent has already committed adultery with her in his heart." This verse highlights the importance of guarding one's thoughts, as sin begins in the heart and mind before it manifests in physical actions. Masturbation often involves lustful thoughts or fantasies, which are inconsistent with the biblical call to purity.

The Apostle Paul further emphasizes the need for self-control and the sanctity of the body in 1 Thessalonians 4:3-5: "For this is the will of God, your sanctification: that you abstain from sexual immorality; that each one of you know how to control his own body in holiness and honor, not in the passion of lust like the Gentiles who do not know God." This passage clearly instructs believers to exercise control over their bodies and to avoid being driven by lustful passions. Masturbation, particularly when it becomes habitual, can undermine self-control and lead to a pattern of behavior that is driven by lust rather than a desire to honor God.

Moreover, the Bible teaches that the body is the temple of the Holy Spirit and should be treated with respect and care. 1 Corinthians 6:19-20 reminds us, "Or do you not know that your body is a temple of the Holy Spirit within you, whom you have from God? You are not your own, for you were bought with a price. So glorify God in your body." Masturbation, when it involves lustful thoughts or becomes a compulsion, can be seen as a misuse of the body that God has given us. Instead of glorifying God, it can lead to feelings of guilt, shame, and spiritual distance.

The secrecy and shame often associated with masturbation are also significant concerns. Ephesians 5:11-12 advises, "Take no part in the unfruitful works of darkness, but instead expose them. For it is shameful even to speak of the things that they do in secret." The hidden nature of masturbation can create a cycle of guilt and secrecy, which isolates individuals from God and others. This secrecy can make it difficult to seek help or accountability, allowing the habit to persist and grow stronger.

The Spiritual Path to Overcoming Masturbation

Overcoming the habit of masturbation requires a deep commitment to purity, self-control, and a renewed focus on honoring God with one's body and mind. This journey involves repentance, renewal of the mind, reliance on God's strength, and engagement in spiritual disciplines.

Repentance is the first step toward breaking free from the habit of masturbation. Repentance involves acknowledging the sin of engaging in lustful thoughts and actions, confessing them to God, and making a deliberate decision to turn away from them. Acts 3:19 calls believers to "Repent therefore, and turn again, that your sins may be blotted out, that times of refreshing may come from the presence of Jehovah." Repentance is not merely about feeling remorseful; it is about taking concrete steps to change behavior and align one's life with God's will.

Renewal of the mind is essential for overcoming the thought patterns that lead to masturbation. Romans 12:2 instructs, "Do not be conformed to this world, but be transformed by the renewal of your mind, that by testing you may discern what is the will of God, what is good and acceptable and perfect." Renewing the mind involves replacing the lies and temptations of the world with the truth of God's Word. This process requires regular meditation on Scripture, prayer, and the rejection of any influences that promote lustful or impure thoughts.

Relying on God's strength is also crucial in the battle against masturbation. Philippians 4:13 reminds us, "I can do all things through him who strengthens me." Overcoming the pull of masturbation requires divine strength, as the flesh is weak and prone to temptation. Consistent, fervent prayer is essential for gaining victory over this habit. Jesus taught His disciples to pray for deliverance from temptation in Matthew 6:13: "And lead us not into temptation, but deliver us from evil." Prayer is a powerful tool for seeking God's help and strength to resist temptation and live in purity.

Engagement in spiritual disciplines, such as prayer, fasting, and Bible study, is necessary for maintaining purity and staying close to God. Galatians 5:16 encourages, "But I say, walk by the Spirit, and you will not gratify the desires of the flesh." Walking by the Spirit involves daily surrender to God, allowing the Holy Spirit to guide and empower you to live in obedience to His Word. This spiritual discipline helps to cultivate a heart that desires holiness and purity, reducing the appeal of sinful behaviors such as masturbation.

Practical Steps to Overcoming Masturbation

In addition to spiritual practices, there are practical steps that can help you break free from the habit of masturbation and maintain a life of purity. These steps include setting boundaries, seeking accountability, developing healthy habits, and addressing underlying issues.

Setting boundaries is a crucial step in overcoming masturbation. Proverbs 4:23 advises, "Keep your heart with all vigilance, for from it flow the springs of life." Protecting your heart and mind from temptation requires setting clear boundaries regarding what you allow yourself to see and engage with. This may involve avoiding websites, movies, or social media platforms that promote sexual content, and being mindful of the environments and situations that trigger temptation. Creating a safe environment that minimizes exposure to sexual content is essential for maintaining purity.

Seeking accountability is another important step in overcoming masturbation. James 5:16 emphasizes the power of accountability: "Therefore, confess your sins to one another and pray for one another, that you may be healed. The prayer of a righteous person has great power as it is working." Having an accountability partner or joining a support group can provide the encouragement, support, and accountability needed to resist temptation and stay on the path of purity. Regular check-ins with someone who understands your struggles can help you stay committed to your goals and provide a safe space for confession and prayer.

Developing healthy habits is also essential in overcoming masturbation. 1 Corinthians 9:27 reflects the importance of discipline: "But I discipline my body and keep it under control, lest after preaching to others I myself should be disqualified." Establishing a routine that includes regular exercise, healthy eating, sufficient rest, and engaging in fulfilling activities can help you reduce stress and avoid the triggers that lead to masturbation. Filling your life with positive, edifying activities can help you break free from the cycle of temptation and sin.

Addressing underlying issues is another key step in overcoming masturbation. Often, masturbation is a coping mechanism for deeper emotional or psychological issues, such as loneliness, stress, depression, or unresolved trauma. Proverbs 20:5 states, "The purpose in a man's heart is like deep water, but a man of understanding will draw it out." Seeking professional counseling or therapy can help you identify and address these underlying issues, providing tools and strategies for healthier ways of coping and healing.

The Role of Prayer and Scripture in Maintaining Purity

Prayer and Scripture are powerful tools in the battle against masturbation, providing strength, guidance, and encouragement to maintain purity. As you seek to overcome this habit, it is important to incorporate both prayer and Scripture into your daily life.

Prayer is central to maintaining purity because it aligns your heart with God's will and invites His power into your life. As you pray, be specific in asking for God's help to resist temptation, to renew your mind, and to live in purity. Psalm 51:10 is a prayer for purity: "Create in me a clean heart, O God, and renew a right spirit within me." Praying for a clean heart and a right spirit is essential in overcoming the pull of masturbation and staying close to God.

In addition to praying for purity, it is important to pray for strength and perseverance. Ephesians 6:10-11 encourages, "Finally, be strong in the Lord and in the strength of his might. Put on the whole armor of God, that you may be able to stand against the schemes of the devil." Prayer is a way to put on the armor of God, asking for His protection and strength to stand firm against the enemy's attacks.

Scripture is another powerful weapon in the battle against masturbation. Hebrews 4:12 describes the power of God's Word: "For the word of God is living and active, sharper than any two-edged sword, piercing to the division of soul and of spirit, of joints and of marrow, and discerning the thoughts and intentions of the heart." Regularly reading, studying, and meditating on Scripture helps to renew your mind, strengthen your spirit, and resist the lies and temptations associated with masturbation.

Memorizing Scripture is also helpful in the fight against masturbation. When tempted, recalling specific verses can help you refocus your mind on God's truth and resist the urge to sin. Psalm 119:11 states, "I have stored up your word in my heart, that I might not sin against you." Storing God's Word in your heart equips you with the truth needed to combat the lies and temptations of masturbation.

Finally, prayer and Scripture should be paired with practical steps to work on behalf of your prayers. James 2:26 reminds us, "For as the body apart from the spirit is dead, so also faith apart from works is dead." True faith is active and involves taking steps to align your actions with your prayers. If you are praying for freedom from masturbation, take practical steps such as setting boundaries, seeking accountability, and developing healthy habits to support your spiritual growth and recovery.

Trusting in God's Power for Long-Term Victory

Overcoming the habit of masturbation is not a one-time event but a lifelong journey that requires ongoing faith, discipline, and reliance on God's strength. Philippians 1:6 offers encouragement: "And I am sure of this, that he who began a good work in you will bring it to completion at the day of Jesus Christ." Trusting in God's power to sustain you is essential in maintaining long-term victory over this habit.

It is also important to continue growing in your faith and relationship with God. Colossians 2:6-7 encourages, "Therefore, as you received Christ Jesus the Lord, so walk in him, rooted and built up in him and established in the faith, just as you were taught, abounding in thanksgiving." Regular prayer, Bible study, and fellowship with other believers are vital for staying spiritually strong and resisting the temptations that can lead to relapse.

In moments of weakness or failure, it is essential to rely on God's grace and forgiveness. 1 John 1:9 offers assurance: "If we confess our sins, he is faithful and just to forgive us our sins and to cleanse us from all unrighteousness." Rather than becoming discouraged by setbacks, you can trust in God's forgiveness and continue to pursue purity with renewed determination.

By applying these biblical principles and practical strategies, you can break free from the self-abuse of masturbation and live a life that honors God. Remember that you are not alone in this journey—God is with you, and He will provide the strength and guidance you need to stay on the path of purity.

CHAPTER 23 How Can We Avoid Homosexuality and Control Same-Sex Attraction Through Biblical Counseling?

Homosexuality and same-sex attraction are challenging topics that require a careful and compassionate approach, especially within the framework of conservative evangelical Christianity. The Bible provides clear teachings on sexual morality, and it is essential to approach this issue with both truth and grace. This chapter will explore the biblical perspective on homosexuality, offer practical and spiritual guidance for those experiencing same-sex attraction, and provide actionable steps for living a life that honors God's design for sexuality.

Understanding Homosexuality from a Biblical Perspective

The Bible is unambiguous in its teaching on homosexuality, consistently affirming that sexual relations are to be confined to the marriage relationship between one man and one woman. This understanding is rooted in the creation account, where Jehovah established the institution of marriage. Genesis 2:24 states, "Therefore a man shall leave his father and his mother and hold fast to his wife, and they shall become one flesh." This foundational text highlights that God's design for sexual intimacy is exclusively within the context of heterosexual marriage.

Leviticus 18:22 and 20:13 explicitly describe homosexual acts as contrary to God's design, stating, "You shall not lie with a male as with a woman; it is an abomination" and "If a man lies with a male as with a woman, both of them have committed an abomination; they shall surely be put to death; their blood is upon them." These verses reflect the seriousness with which God views sexual immorality, including homosexual behavior.

The New Testament also addresses homosexuality, with the Apostle Paul reaffirming the Old Testament teachings in Romans 1:26-27: "For this reason God gave them up to dishonorable passions. For their women exchanged natural relations for those that are contrary to nature; and the men likewise gave up natural relations with women and were consumed with passion for one another, men committing shameless acts with men and receiving in themselves the due penalty for their error." Paul's writings clarify that homosexual behavior is inconsistent with God's design for human sexuality.

1 Corinthians 6:9-10 further emphasizes that those who practice homosexuality, among other sins, will not inherit the kingdom of God: " Or do you not know that the unrighteous will not inherit the kingdom of God? Do not be deceived; neither fornicators, nor idolaters, nor adulterers, nor men of passive homosexual acts,[1] nor men of active homosexual acts, nor thieves, nor greedy persons, nor drunkards, nor revilers, nor swindlers, will inherit the kingdom of God." However, the passage continues with a message of hope in verse 11: "And such were some of you. But you were washed, you were sanctified, you were justified in the name of the Lord Jesus Christ and by the Spirit of our God." This verse highlights the transformative power of God's grace, emphasizing that change is possible for those who seek to live in accordance with God's will.

The Spiritual Path to Overcoming Same-Sex Attraction

For those who experience same-sex attraction, the journey toward living in alignment with biblical teaching can be challenging. It requires a commitment to spiritual growth, self-control, and reliance on God's

[1] The two Greek terms refer to passive men partners and active men partners in consensual homosexual acts. "nor men of passive homosexual acts **[μαλακοὶ]**, nor men of active homosexual acts **[ἀρσενοκοῖται]**"

strength. This journey involves repentance, renewal of the mind, and engagement in spiritual disciplines.

Repentance is the first step toward overcoming same-sex attraction. Repentance involves acknowledging that acting on same-sex desires is inconsistent with God's design for human sexuality. It is a commitment to turn away from these desires and seek God's will. Acts 3:19 calls believers to "Repent therefore, and turn again, that your sins may be blotted out, that times of refreshing may come from the presence of Jehovah." Repentance is not merely about rejecting homosexual behavior; it is about a wholehearted return to God's design for sexuality.

Renewal of the mind is essential in overcoming same-sex attraction. Romans 12:2 instructs, "Do not be conformed to this world, but be transformed by the renewal of your mind, that by testing you may discern what is the will of God, what is good and acceptable and perfect." The renewal of the mind involves rejecting the world's messages that normalize or celebrate homosexuality and instead filling the mind with God's truth. This process requires regular engagement with Scripture, prayer, and the rejection of any influences that promote unbiblical views of sexuality.

Relying on God's strength is crucial in the battle against same-sex attraction. Philippians 4:13 reminds us, "I can do all things through him who strengthens me." Overcoming same-sex attraction requires divine strength, as human willpower alone is insufficient. Consistent, fervent prayer is essential for gaining victory over these desires. Jesus taught His disciples to pray for deliverance from temptation in Matthew 6:13: "And lead us not into temptation, but deliver us from evil." Prayer is a powerful tool for seeking God's help and strength to resist temptation and live in purity.

Engagement in spiritual disciplines, such as prayer, fasting, and Bible study, is necessary for maintaining purity and staying close to God. Galatians 5:16 encourages, "But I say, walk by the Spirit, and you will not gratify the desires of the flesh." Walking by the Spirit involves daily surrender to God, allowing the Holy Spirit to guide and empower you to live in obedience to His Word. This spiritual discipline helps to cultivate a heart that desires holiness and purity, reducing the appeal of sinful behaviors.

Practical Steps to Avoiding Homosexual Behavior and Controlling Same-Sex Attraction

In addition to spiritual practices, there are practical steps that can help you avoid homosexual behavior and control same-sex attraction. These steps include setting boundaries, seeking accountability, developing healthy relationships, and addressing underlying issues.

Setting boundaries is a crucial step in avoiding homosexual behavior. Proverbs 4:23 advises, "Keep your heart with all vigilance, for from it flow the springs of life." Protecting your heart and mind from temptation requires setting clear boundaries regarding the situations, relationships, and environments you allow yourself to be in. This may involve avoiding close friendships with individuals who may influence you toward same-sex behavior, as well as being mindful of the media and entertainment you consume that might normalize or promote homosexuality.

Seeking accountability is another important step in controlling same-sex attraction. James 5:16 emphasizes the power of accountability: "Therefore, confess your sins to one another and pray for one another, that you may be healed. The prayer of a righteous person has great power as it is working." Having an accountability partner or joining a support group can provide the encouragement, support, and accountability needed to resist temptation and stay on the path of purity. Regular check-ins with someone who understands your struggles can help you stay committed to your goals and provide a safe space for confession and prayer.

Developing healthy relationships is also essential in avoiding homosexual behavior. 1 Corinthians 15:33 warns, "Do not be deceived: 'Bad company ruins good morals.'" Surrounding yourself with godly friends and mentors who encourage you to live according to biblical principles can help you stay strong in your commitment to purity. Developing close, non-romantic friendships with others of the same gender can also fulfill the need for companionship and emotional support in a healthy and biblical way.

Addressing underlying issues is another key step in overcoming same-sex attraction. Often, same-sex attraction can be linked to deeper emotional or psychological issues, such as past trauma, unmet needs for love and affirmation, or identity confusion. Proverbs 20:5 states, "The purpose in a man's heart is like deep water, but a man of understanding will draw it out." Seeking professional counseling or therapy can help you identify and address these underlying issues, providing tools and strategies for healthier ways of coping and healing.

The Role of Prayer and Scripture in Maintaining Purity

Prayer and Scripture are powerful tools in the battle against same-sex attraction, providing strength, guidance, and encouragement to maintain purity. As you seek to live in alignment with biblical teachings on sexuality, it is important to incorporate both prayer and Scripture into your daily life.

Prayer is central to maintaining purity because it aligns your heart with God's will and invites His power into your life. As you pray, be specific in asking for God's help to resist temptation, to renew your mind, and to live in purity. Psalm 51:10 is a prayer for purity: "Create in me a clean heart, O God, and renew a right spirit within me." Praying for a clean heart and a right spirit is essential in overcoming the pull of same-sex attraction and staying close to God.

In addition to praying for purity, it is important to pray for strength and perseverance. Ephesians 6:10-11 encourages, "Finally, be strong in the Lord and in the strength of his might. Put on the whole armor of God, that you may be able to stand against the schemes of the devil." Prayer is a way to put on the armor of God, asking for His protection and strength to stand firm against the enemy's attacks.

Scripture is another powerful weapon in the battle against same-sex attraction. Hebrews 4:12 describes the power of God's Word: "For the word of God is living and active, sharper than any two-edged sword, piercing to the division of soul and of spirit, of joints and of marrow, and discerning the thoughts and intentions of the heart." Regularly reading, studying, and meditating on Scripture helps to renew your mind, strengthen your spirit, and resist the lies and temptations associated with homosexuality.

Memorizing Scripture is also helpful in the fight against same-sex attraction. When tempted, recalling specific verses can help you refocus your mind on God's truth and resist the urge to sin. Psalm 119:11 states, "I have stored up your word in my heart, that I might not sin against you." Storing God's Word in your heart equips you with the truth needed to combat the lies and temptations of homosexuality.

Walking in God's Grace and Strength

Overcoming same-sex attraction and avoiding homosexual behavior is not easy, but with God's grace and strength, it is possible. It is important to remember that you are not alone in this journey—God is with you, and He is ready to provide the help and guidance you need to live in purity.

Relying on God's grace is crucial in this process. 2 Corinthians 12:9 offers encouragement: "But he said to me, 'My grace is sufficient for you, for my power is made perfect in weakness.' Therefore I will boast all the more gladly of my weaknesses, so that the power of Christ may rest upon me." God's grace is sufficient to help you overcome the weaknesses associated with same-sex attraction, and His power is made perfect in your weakness.

It is also important to walk in the strength that God provides. Philippians 4:13 reminds us, "I can do all things through him who strengthens me." God's strength is available to you as you commit to living according to His design for sexuality. Daily reliance on His strength, rather than your own, will help you stay on the path of purity and resist temptation.

It is essential to trust in God's faithfulness to complete the work He has begun in you. Philippians 1:6 encourages, "And I am sure of this, that he who began a good work in you will bring it to completion at the day of Jesus Christ." Trusting in God's faithfulness means believing that He will continue to work in your life, helping you to grow in purity and obedience to His Word.

Avoiding homosexuality and controlling same-sex attraction requires a combination of spiritual practices, practical steps, and reliance on God's grace and strength. By applying these biblical principles, you can overcome the challenges associated with same-sex attraction and live a life that honors God's design for sexuality.

How Can We Avoid Homosexuality and Control Same-Sex Attraction Through Cultivating Self-Control?

What Is Self-Control?

Self-control is the ability to regulate one's thoughts, emotions, and actions in alignment with biblical principles rather than being led by the desires of the flesh or worldly influences. It is an essential aspect of Christian life that involves the conscious decision to live according to God's will rather than succumbing to temptations or sinful impulses. As the apostle Paul wrote, "But the fruit of the Spirit is love, joy, peace, patience, kindness, goodness, faithfulness, gentleness, self-control; against such things, there is no law" (Galatians 5:22-23). Self-control is not merely a human effort but a manifestation of the Holy Spirit's work in a believer's life.

Why Is Self-Control Essential?

Self-control is vital for every Christian because it is foundational to living a life that pleases Jehovah. Without self-control, believers can easily be swayed by sinful desires and the temptations of the world. Proverbs 25:28 warns, "A man without self-control is like a city broken into and left without walls." This vivid imagery highlights the vulnerability of a life without self-control, where one is exposed to the assaults of sin and the influence of Satan.

Moreover, self-control is essential because it is directly related to our spiritual maturity and growth. Hebrews 5:14 explains, "But solid food is for the mature, for those who have their powers of discernment trained by constant practice to distinguish good from evil." This maturity, which comes through self-control, enables us to discern right from wrong and make decisions that honor God. For those struggling with same-sex attraction, self-control is particularly crucial as it helps them resist temptations and align their desires with God's will.

Why Is Self-Control Such a Challenge?

The challenge of self-control stems from the inherent sinful nature of humanity. Genesis 6:5 and 8:21 describe the condition of the human heart as being "only evil continually" and "from youth," indicating the deep-rooted inclination towards sin. Jeremiah 17:9 further emphasizes this by stating, "The heart is deceitful above all things, and desperately sick; who can understand it?" The apostle Paul, in Romans 7:21-25, expresses the inner conflict experienced by every believer: "So I find it to be a law that when I want to do right, evil lies close at hand. For I delight in the law of God, in my inner being, but I see in my members another law waging war against the law of my mind and making me captive to the law of sin that dwells in my members."

This struggle highlights the ongoing battle between the flesh and the spirit. Even with the desire to do what is right, the flesh pulls us towards sin, making self-control a constant challenge. For individuals dealing with same-sex attraction, this struggle can be even more intense, as the desires may feel natural or intrinsic, yet they must be controlled to live in obedience to God's Word.

How to Cultivate Self-Control

Cultivating self-control is a process that requires intentional effort, prayer, and reliance on God's Word. Here's how one can develop this crucial virtue:

Pray for the Holy Spirit-Inspired Word to Get Down into Your Heart

The first step in cultivating self-control is to pray that the Holy Spirit-inspired Word penetrates your heart. This is essential because the Word of God is "living and active, sharper than any two-edged sword" (Hebrews 4:12). It has the power to transform our hearts and minds, aligning our desires with God's will. By allowing the Scriptures to dwell richly in us, our love for God and His Word can become greater than our sinful desires.

Act on Behalf of the Prayer

Prayer is essential, but it must be coupled with action. After praying for God's Word to impact your heart, actively seek out scriptural counsel that can help you succeed in cultivating self-control. This involves researching and studying relevant passages, then formulating a practical plan to apply those principles in your daily life. For example, if you struggle with lustful thoughts, you might meditate on Job 31:1, where Job says, "I have made a covenant with my eyes; how then could I gaze at a virgin?" By committing to avoid situations that trigger sinful desires, you act on behalf of your prayer.

Feed on God's Word Regularly

Regular and meaningful Bible study is crucial in developing self-control. Jesus said, "Man shall not live by bread alone, but by every word that comes from the mouth of God" (Matthew 4:4). Just as physical food nourishes the body, spiritual food—God's Word—nourishes the soul and strengthens the believer's resolve to resist temptation. Consistent study of the Bible helps to internalize God's commandments, making it easier to exercise self-control in moments of weakness.

How Can Bible Study Help You Develop Self-Control?

Bible study provides the knowledge and wisdom necessary to navigate life's challenges. By immersing yourself in Scripture, you gain insights into God's character and His expectations for your life. This understanding helps you to identify areas where self-control is needed and provides practical guidance on how to develop it. For instance, studying passages like 1 Corinthians 10:13, which assures us that "No temptation has overtaken you that is not common to man. God is faithful, and he will not let you be tempted beyond your ability, but with the temptation he will also provide the way of escape, that you may be able to endure it," can empower you to resist temptations by recognizing that God always provides a way out.

If We Fail to Exercise Self-Control

Despite our best efforts, there will be times when we fail to exercise self-control. When this happens, feelings of shame and guilt may overwhelm us, making us hesitant to approach Jehovah in prayer. However, this is precisely when we need to seek Him the most. The psalmist's prayer in Psalm 51:9-11 is a model for us: "Hide your face from my sins, and blot out all my iniquities. Create in me a clean heart, O God, and renew a right spirit within me. Cast me not away from your presence, and take not your Holy Spirit from me." When we fail, we should immediately go to Jehovah, beg for His forgiveness, and seek His help to overcome future temptations.

Jehovah promises not to despise our sincere prayers for mercy. Psalm 102:17 reminds us, "He regards the prayer of the destitute and does not despise their prayer." Additionally, the apostle John offers comfort in 1 John 1:7: "But if we walk in the light, as he is in the light, we have fellowship with one another, and the blood of Jesus his Son cleanses us from all sin." Even when we falter, we can be confident that Jehovah, in His mercy, will forgive us if we are truly repentant. Jesus instructed us to forgive repeatedly, and we can be assured that Jehovah will do the same for us, as seen in Matthew 18:21-22 and Colossians 3:13.

What Does It Mean to Cultivate Self-Control?

Cultivating self-control involves a deliberate and ongoing effort to align one's desires and actions with God's will. It is a process that requires both the denial of sinful impulses and the active pursuit of righteousness. Self-control starts in the heart, where our affections and desires reside. Jesus taught that it is "out of the abundance of the heart that the mouth speaks" (Matthew 12:34). Therefore, cultivating self-control begins with examining and reshaping our hearts through the power of God's Word.

Where Does Self-Control Start?

Self-control starts with the mind. Romans 12:2 urges, "Do not be conformed to this world, but be transformed by the renewal of your mind, that by testing you may discern what is the will of God, what is good and acceptable and perfect." The renewal of the mind through Scripture is the foundation of self-control. When our minds are filled with God's truth, we can better resist the lies and temptations that seek to lead us astray.

Why Is Self-Control Important for Christians to Cultivate?

Self-control is crucial for Christians because it is a reflection of spiritual maturity and a necessary quality for living a life that pleases God. Without self-control, a believer is vulnerable to sin and unable to fully experience the freedom that comes from living in obedience to Christ. Additionally, self-control is a witness to others of the transforming power of the Gospel. Titus 2:11-12 states, "For the grace of God has appeared, bringing salvation for all people, training us to renounce ungodliness and worldly passions, and to live self-controlled, upright, and godly lives in the present age."

Why Is Self-Control Particularly Challenging for Some?

For some individuals, self-control may be particularly challenging due to various factors, including past experiences, personality traits, or deeply ingrained habits. The sinful nature, described in Galatians 5:17 as "the desires of the flesh," is in constant opposition to the desires of the Spirit, making the exercise of self-control a daily battle. Those struggling with same-sex attraction may find self-control especially difficult because the desires can feel intrinsic or unchangeable. However, Scripture assures us that "I can do all things through him who strengthens me" (Philippians 4:13), providing hope that with God's help, even the most challenging battles can be won.

Why Is Self-Control Necessary for Those Struggling with Same-Sex Attraction?

For individuals struggling with same-sex attraction, self-control is necessary to live in accordance with God's design for sexuality. The Bible teaches that sexual relations are intended for marriage between one man and one woman (Genesis 2:24; Matthew 19:4-6). Therefore, acting on same-sex attraction would be contrary to God's will. Cultivating self-control helps individuals resist temptations and align their actions with biblical truth, thereby living a life that honors God.

Why Is Self-Control a Quality That We Can Help One Another Cultivate?

Self-control is not cultivated in isolation. As members of the body of Christ, believers are called to support and encourage one another in their spiritual growth. Hebrews 10:24-25 exhorts us to "consider how to stir up one another to love and good works, not neglecting to meet together, as is the habit of some, but encouraging one another, and all the more as you see the Day drawing near." By holding each other accountable, praying for one another, and offering practical support, Christians can help one another develop the self-control necessary to live godly lives.

Become Full-Grown Through Self-Control

Spiritual maturity is marked by the development of self-control. A lack of self-control indicates that we are still spiritual infants, unable to fully comprehend and apply the teachings of Scripture. The apostle Paul admonishes us to "become mature in your understanding" (1 Corinthians 14:20). The goal of every believer is to "attain to the unity of the faith and of the knowledge of the Son of God, to mature manhood, to the measure of the stature of the fullness of Christ" (Ephesians 4:13). This maturity enables us to stand firm in the face of false teachings and deceit, fully grounded in the truth of God's Word.

Reverential Fear of God and Hating What Is Bad

A reverential fear of God and a hatred for what is evil are essential components of self-control. Proverbs 8:13 declares, "The fear of Jehovah is hatred of evil. Pride and arrogance and the way of evil and perverted speech I hate." When we have a deep respect and awe for God, we are motivated to obey Him and avoid sin. This fear of God is not a paralyzing fear but a healthy recognition of His holiness and justice. It leads to a sincere desire to live in a way that pleases Him, which includes exercising self-control.

Unselfish Love Helps

Unselfish love, as described in 1 Corinthians 13, is another key factor in developing self-control. Love "does not insist on its own way; it is not irritable or resentful" (1 Corinthians 13:5). When we love others selflessly, we are more likely to put their needs above our own desires, which helps us to practice self-control. This love is a reflection of the love that God has shown us through Christ, who "gave himself up for us, a fragrant offering and sacrifice to God" (Ephesians 5:2). By cultivating this kind of love, we can better resist selfish impulses and live in a way that honors God and serves others.

Faith and Humility as Helpers

Faith and humility are indispensable helpers in the cultivation of self-control. Faith in God's promises gives us the confidence to resist temptations, knowing that He is faithful and will provide the strength we need. Hebrews 11:6 reminds us that "without faith it is impossible to please him, for whoever would draw near to God must believe that he exists and that he rewards those who seek him." Humility, on the other hand, allows us to recognize our dependence on God and our need for His grace in overcoming sin. James 4:6-7 states, "God opposes the proud but gives grace to the humble. Submit yourselves therefore to God. Resist the devil, and he will flee from you."

How Can We Deprogram Our Mind That Is Bent Toward Evil Desires?

Deprogramming a mind that is bent toward evil desires requires a complete renewal of the mind through Scripture. Romans 12:2 exhorts us, "Do not be conformed to this world, but be transformed by the renewal of your mind, that by testing you may discern what is the will of God, what is good and acceptable and perfect." This transformation involves replacing worldly thoughts with godly thoughts, which is accomplished through regular meditation on Scripture, prayer, and the application of biblical principles in daily life.

What You Should Know

Today's culture often undermines self-control, promoting a message of instant gratification and the pursuit of personal desires without regard for moral or spiritual consequences. However, early learning of self-control is vital for spiritual growth and maturity. The cost of not learning self-control can be heavy, leading to spiritual, emotional, and relational damage.

To cultivate self-control, it is important to teach oneself about consequences and to create incentives for positive behavior. Patience is also essential, as the development of self-control is a gradual process. Success and positive behavior should be rewarded, reinforcing the habit of self-control.

Self-Control Includes the Ability to:

- **Delay Gratification**: The ability to wait for a greater reward rather than giving in to immediate desires.
- **Restrain Impulses**: The discipline to say no to temptations that contradict biblical principles.
- **Put Others Before Self**: The willingness to prioritize the needs of others above one's own desires, reflecting the selfless love of Christ.

By cultivating these aspects of self-control, Christians can successfully avoid homosexuality and control same-sex attraction, living a life that honors Jehovah and reflects the transforming power of His Word.

CHAPTER 24 How Can the Bible Help Us Cope with Loneliness?

Understanding the Nature and Roots of Loneliness

Loneliness is a multifaceted experience that extends beyond mere physical isolation. It can occur even when surrounded by people, manifesting as an emotional and psychological state where an individual feels disconnected, misunderstood, or alienated from others. Loneliness can stem from various sources, such as life transitions, loss of a loved one, social rejection, or chronic illness. Understanding the nature of loneliness is the first step in addressing it effectively.

The Bible recognizes the deep human need for connection and companionship. From the beginning, Jehovah acknowledged, "It is not good that the man should be alone" (Genesis 2:18). This statement reflects the intrinsic social nature of human beings, created in the image of a relational God. Therefore, when that need for connection is unmet, it can lead to feelings of loneliness, which the Bible addresses through both spiritual and practical means.

The Spiritual Dimension of Loneliness

Loneliness is not only an emotional state but also a spiritual one. It can arise when there is a perceived or real distance between oneself and God. This spiritual loneliness can be more profound than physical loneliness, as it touches the core of one's being. In moments of spiritual desolation, it is vital to remember that Jehovah is always present, even when He seems distant. Psalm 139:7-10 offers reassurance: "Where shall I go from your Spirit? Or where shall I flee from your presence? If I ascend to heaven, you are there! If I make my bed in Sheol, you are there! If I take the wings of the morning and dwell in the uttermost parts of the sea, even there your hand shall lead me, and your right hand shall hold me."

This passage highlights the omnipresence of God, emphasizing that no matter how isolated one feels, Jehovah is near. Cultivating an awareness of God's constant presence is a powerful antidote to loneliness, transforming it from a burden into an opportunity for deepened spiritual intimacy.

Biblical Examples of Overcoming Loneliness

The Bible provides numerous examples of individuals who faced profound loneliness yet found solace in their relationship with Jehovah. These stories serve as both encouragement and instruction for those dealing with similar feelings today.

1. David's Loneliness in the Wilderness

David, before becoming king, experienced intense loneliness as he fled from Saul. Despite being surrounded by men who followed him, David's psalms reveal a deep sense of isolation and a longing for God. In Psalm 142:4-5, he writes, "Look to the right and see: there is none who takes notice of me; no refuge remains to me; no one cares for my soul. I cry to you, O Jehovah; I say, 'You are my refuge, my portion in the land of the living.'"

David's response to his loneliness was to cry out to Jehovah, acknowledging Him as his refuge. This teaches that in moments of loneliness, turning to God in prayer and seeking His presence can provide the comfort and strength needed to endure.

2. Elijah's Despair and Divine Encounter

The prophet Elijah also experienced loneliness, especially after his victory over the prophets of Baal when he fled from Jezebel's wrath. In 1 Kings 19:4, Elijah, overwhelmed with despair, asks Jehovah to take his life. Yet, in his isolation, Elijah encounters Jehovah in a still, small voice, reminding him that he is not alone. God reassures Elijah that there are still seven thousand in Israel who have not bowed to Baal (1 Kings 19:18).

This narrative illustrates that loneliness can cloud our perception, making us feel more isolated than we are. However, Jehovah's response to Elijah shows that God is always aware of our circumstances and will provide the reassurance and guidance we need.

3. Jesus' Loneliness in Gethsemane

Jesus Christ, the Son of God, experienced profound loneliness, especially in the Garden of Gethsemane. As He faced the prospect of crucifixion, He asked His disciples to stay awake and pray with Him, but they fell asleep (Matthew 26:40). In His moment of deepest anguish, Jesus turned to His Father, praying earnestly for strength. Luke 22:44 records, "And being in agony he prayed more earnestly; and his sweat became like great drops of blood falling down to the ground."

Jesus' response to loneliness was to seek communion with His Father, demonstrating the importance of prayer in moments of isolation. His example teaches us to rely on our relationship with Jehovah during times of loneliness, knowing that God is always present and ready to provide comfort.

The Christian Community as a Remedy for Loneliness

One of the primary ways the Bible addresses loneliness is through the Christian community, which is meant to be a family where each member feels valued and connected. The early Christian church is depicted as a close-knit community where believers shared their lives, supported one another, and fostered a sense of belonging. Acts 2:44-47 describes how "all who believed were together and had all things in common. And they were selling their possessions and belongings and distributing the proceeds to all, as any had need. And day by day, attending the temple together and breaking bread in their homes, they received their food with glad and generous hearts, praising God and having favor with all the people."

This passage highlights the importance of fellowship and mutual support in overcoming loneliness. The Christian congregation is intended to be a place of refuge and connection, where believers can experience the love of Christ through their relationships with one another.

1. Building Meaningful Relationships

To combat loneliness, it is essential to actively build relationships within the Christian community. Hebrews 10:24-25 encourages believers not to neglect meeting together but to spur one another on toward love and good deeds. Regular participation in congregational activities, small groups, and ministry work fosters a sense of belonging and provides opportunities to form deep, meaningful connections.

However, building relationships requires effort and intentionality. Proverbs 18:24 states, "A man who has friends must himself be friendly, but there is a friend who sticks closer than a brother." This proverb emphasizes the importance of taking the initiative to reach out to others, showing hospitality, and being willing to invest time and energy into relationships.

2. Serving Others as an Antidote to Loneliness

Service to others is another powerful way to overcome loneliness. Jesus taught that true fulfillment comes from serving others: "It is more blessed to give than to receive" (Acts 20:35). When we focus on meeting the needs of others, we shift our attention away from our own loneliness and create opportunities for connection and community.

Volunteering in the church, helping those in need, or simply offering a listening ear to someone going through a difficult time can provide a sense of purpose and belonging. Serving others not only alleviates loneliness but also deepens our relationship with Jehovah, as we emulate Christ's example of selfless love.

3. The Role of Mentorship and Discipleship

Mentorship and discipleship are crucial aspects of the Christian community that can help combat loneliness. Paul's relationship with Timothy serves as a model of mentorship, where Paul provided guidance, support, and encouragement to Timothy in his faith journey. In 2 Timothy 1:2, Paul addresses Timothy as "my beloved child," indicating the close, familial bond they shared.

Being mentored by a mature Christian can provide the support and accountability needed to navigate loneliness, while mentoring others allows for the development of meaningful, reciprocal relationships. Discipleship creates a sense of purpose and connection within the body of Christ, fostering a supportive environment where loneliness is less likely to take root.

Practical Strategies for Overcoming Loneliness

While the Bible provides spiritual solutions to loneliness, it also encourages practical steps that individuals can take to address their situation. These strategies are designed to help readers actively work on behalf of their prayers for connection and companionship.

1. Deepening Your Relationship with God Through Prayer and Study

The most crucial strategy for overcoming loneliness is to deepen your relationship with Jehovah through consistent prayer and Bible study. Philippians 4:6-7 reminds us, "Do not be anxious about anything, but in every situation, by prayer and petition, with thanksgiving, present your requests to God. And the peace of God, which transcends all understanding, will guard your hearts and your minds in Christ Jesus."

Prayer is not only a way to communicate with God but also a means of drawing near to Him and experiencing His presence. By presenting your loneliness to Jehovah and asking for His guidance and comfort, you invite His peace into your life. Regular Bible study further strengthens this relationship, as it allows you to immerse yourself in God's promises and gain a deeper understanding of His love and faithfulness.

2. Engaging in Fellowship and Building Community

Actively participating in church activities and small groups is vital in combating loneliness. Hebrews 10:24-25 encourages believers to meet together regularly for mutual encouragement and support. By engaging in fellowship, you create opportunities for connection and develop a network of relationships that can provide emotional and spiritual support.

If you find it difficult to connect with others, consider joining or starting a small group focused on shared interests, such as Bible study, prayer, or community service. Small groups offer a more intimate setting where meaningful relationships can flourish. Additionally, volunteering for church ministries or outreach programs provides opportunities to serve alongside others, fostering camaraderie and a sense of belonging.

3. Focusing on Personal Growth and Purpose

Loneliness can often be alleviated by focusing on personal growth and pursuing your God-given purpose. Ephesians 2:10 reminds us, "For we are his workmanship, created in Christ Jesus for good works, which God prepared beforehand, that we should walk in them." Engaging in activities that align with your purpose, whether it be ministry, creative endeavors, or learning new skills, helps you build a fulfilling life that mitigates the effects of loneliness.

Setting goals for personal development, such as learning a new language, pursuing further education, or developing a talent, provides a sense of direction and accomplishment. These pursuits not only occupy your time but also build your confidence and self-worth, making it easier to connect with others.

4. Practicing Gratitude and Contentment

Gratitude is a powerful antidote to loneliness, as it shifts your focus from what is lacking to what is present. 1 Thessalonians 5:18 encourages believers to "give thanks in all circumstances; for this is God's will for you in Christ Jesus." By cultivating an attitude of gratitude, you can change your perspective on loneliness, recognizing the blessings in your life and fostering a sense of contentment.

Practicing gratitude can be as simple as keeping a daily journal where you record things for which you are thankful. Over time, this practice helps you develop a more positive outlook, reducing the emotional impact of loneliness and increasing your overall sense of well-being.

5. Serving Others as a Way to Combat Loneliness

As mentioned earlier, service is a powerful way to overcome loneliness. By focusing on the needs of others, you not only alleviate your own loneliness but also build connections and foster community. Jesus' example of service is a model for all believers to follow: "For even the Son of Man came not to be served but to serve, and to give his life as a ransom for many" (Mark 10:45).

Look for opportunities to serve in your church or community, whether through volunteer work, mentoring, or simply offering a helping hand to someone in need. Acts of service not only provide a sense of purpose but also create bonds with others that can alleviate feelings of isolation.

6. Cultivating a Positive Mindset

Loneliness can often lead to negative thought patterns, such as feelings of worthlessness or hopelessness. The Bible encourages believers to renew their minds and focus on what is true, noble, right, pure, lovely, and admirable (Philippians 4:8). By cultivating a positive mindset, you can combat the negative effects of loneliness and develop a more resilient and hopeful outlook on life.

To cultivate a positive mindset, practice mindfulness and meditation on Scripture, focusing on God's promises and truths. Replace negative thoughts with affirmations grounded in Scripture, such as "I am fearfully and wonderfully made" (Psalm 139:14) and " Jehovah is my shepherd; I shall not want" (Psalm 23:1). Over time, this practice will help you develop a more positive and resilient mindset, reducing the impact of loneliness.

Overcoming the Spiritual and Psychological Roots of Loneliness

While practical strategies are essential in addressing loneliness, it is also important to address the spiritual and psychological roots of loneliness. Often, loneliness can stem from unresolved emotional or spiritual issues, such as past trauma, unforgiveness, or a lack of self-worth. Addressing these underlying issues is crucial for long-term healing and growth.

1. Healing from Past Wounds

Many people experience loneliness as a result of past wounds or trauma. Whether it be the loss of a loved one, a broken relationship, or a painful childhood experience, these wounds can create emotional barriers that prevent connection and lead to feelings of isolation. Isaiah 61:1 offers hope for healing: "The Spirit of Jehovah God is upon me, because Jehovah has anointed me to bring good news to the poor; he has sent me to bind up the brokenhearted, to proclaim liberty to the captives, and the opening of the prison to those who are bound."

Seeking healing from past wounds may involve prayer, counseling, or support from trusted friends or mentors. It is important to bring these wounds before Jehovah, asking for His healing and guidance. As you heal, you will find it easier to connect with others and build meaningful relationships.

2. Forgiving Others and Yourself

Unforgiveness can be a significant barrier to overcoming loneliness, as it creates emotional distance and prevents reconciliation. Ephesians 4:32 instructs believers, "Be kind to one another, tenderhearted, forgiving one another, as God in Christ forgave you." Forgiving others and yourself is a crucial step in healing from loneliness and building healthy relationships.

Forgiveness does not mean condoning wrong behavior or allowing others to continue harming you. Instead, it involves releasing the burden of anger and resentment, allowing Jehovah to bring justice and healing. As you forgive, you open the door to reconciliation and deeper connection with others.

3. Developing a Healthy Self-Worth

A lack of self-worth can contribute to loneliness, as it leads to feelings of inadequacy and fear of rejection. The Bible teaches that every person is valuable and loved by Jehovah, created in His image with a unique purpose. Psalm 139:13-14 affirms, "For you formed my inward parts; you knitted me together in my mother's womb. I praise you, for I am fearfully and wonderfully made."

Developing a healthy self-worth involves understanding and accepting your identity in Christ. Regularly meditate on Scriptures that affirm your worth and value in God's eyes, such as Ephesians 2:10 and 1 Peter 2:9. As you grow in your understanding of your identity in Christ, you will gain the confidence needed to form and maintain meaningful relationships.

4. Addressing Spiritual Loneliness

As mentioned earlier, spiritual loneliness can occur when there is a perceived or real distance between oneself and God. Addressing this form of loneliness involves renewing your relationship with Jehovah through prayer, worship, and Bible study. James 4:8 encourages, "Draw near to God, and he will draw near to you." This promise assures that as you seek to deepen your relationship with God, He will respond by drawing near to you.

In addition to personal prayer and study, consider engaging in corporate worship and spiritual disciplines, such as fasting and meditation. These practices help to cultivate a deeper awareness of Jehovah's presence and foster spiritual intimacy, alleviating feelings of spiritual loneliness.

The Role of Christian Counseling in Overcoming Loneliness

While Scripture and spiritual practices provide profound support in overcoming loneliness, there may be times when professional counseling is also beneficial. Proverbs 11:14 advises, "Where there is no guidance, a people falls, but in an abundance of counselors there is safety." Seeking help from a qualified Christian counselor can provide additional tools and strategies for coping with loneliness, especially if it is linked to deeper psychological issues, such as depression or anxiety.

Christian counseling integrates biblical principles with psychological practices, providing a holistic approach to healing. A counselor can help you identify and address the underlying causes of loneliness, develop healthy coping strategies, and build a support network within the Christian community.

Perseverance and Trust in Jehovah's Plan

Overcoming loneliness is often a journey that requires perseverance and trust in Jehovah's plan. James 1:2-4 encourages believers to consider trials, including loneliness, as opportunities for growth: "Count it all joy, my brothers, when you meet trials of various kinds, for you know that the testing of your faith produces steadfastness. And let steadfastness have its full effect, that you may be perfect and complete, lacking in nothing."

Perseverance involves continuing to seek God's presence, engage in community, and serve others, even when the results are not immediate. Trusting in Jehovah's timing and plan is essential, as He often uses seasons of loneliness to refine our character, deepen our faith, and prepare us for future blessings.

Remember that Jehovah is always with you, even in your loneliest moments, and His Word provides the guidance and comfort needed to navigate this challenge. By applying the principles outlined in this chapter and relying on Jehovah's strength, you can overcome loneliness and experience the fullness of life that He intends for you.

CHAPTER 25 How Can We Deal with Spiritual Sicknesses of Mind and Heart?

Understanding Spiritual Sickness: A Biblical Perspective

Spiritual sickness is a condition that affects both the mind and the heart, leading to a disconnection from Jehovah, weakened faith, and compromised spiritual well-being. This condition is not merely a result of external circumstances but often stems from internal struggles, such as unresolved sin, bitterness, lack of faith, or neglect of spiritual disciplines. Spiritual sickness can manifest in various forms, including depression, anxiety, apathy, resentment, and a general sense of hopelessness. It is essential to recognize the symptoms of spiritual sickness early on to address them effectively and restore spiritual health.

The Bible provides numerous examples of individuals who faced spiritual sickness and how they overcame it through God's guidance. For instance, King David experienced profound spiritual sickness after his sin with Bathsheba, leading to deep remorse and a sense of separation from Jehovah. In Psalm 32:3-4, David describes the physical and emotional toll of unconfessed sin: "When I kept silent, my bones wasted away through my groaning all day long. For day and night your hand was heavy upon me; my strength was dried up as by the heat of summer." This passage highlights the interconnectedness of spiritual and physical health and the importance of addressing spiritual sickness promptly.

The Root Causes of Spiritual Sickness

To effectively deal with spiritual sickness, it is crucial to identify and understand its root causes. These causes can vary widely but often include the following:

1. Unconfessed Sin and Guilt

Unconfessed sin is one of the primary causes of spiritual sickness. When a believer harbors sin without repentance, it creates a barrier between them and Jehovah, leading to feelings of guilt, shame, and spiritual desolation. Psalm 66:18 states, "If I had wickedness in my heart, Jehovah would not have listened." This verse underscores the impact of unrepented sin on one's relationship with God and the importance of confession and repentance in restoring spiritual health.

2. Bitterness and Unforgiveness

Bitterness and unforgiveness can also contribute to spiritual sickness, poisoning the heart and mind. Hebrews 12:15 warns, "See to it that no one fails to obtain the grace of God; that no 'root of bitterness' springs up and causes trouble, and by it many become defiled." Bitterness can fester when unresolved conflicts or hurts are allowed to linger, leading to spiritual and emotional decay. Forgiveness, both of others and oneself, is essential for healing and spiritual restoration.

3. Neglect of Spiritual Disciplines

Another common cause of spiritual sickness is the neglect of spiritual disciplines, such as prayer, Bible study, worship, and fellowship. These practices are vital for maintaining a healthy relationship with Jehovah and for spiritual growth. When they are neglected, believers can become spiritually malnourished, leading to feelings of emptiness, apathy, and disconnection from God. Revelation 2:4-5 admonishes the church in Ephesus for abandoning their first love and calls them to repent and return to the practices they once held dear: "But I have this against you, that you have abandoned the love you had at first. Remember therefore from where you have fallen; repent, and do the works you did at first."

4. Lack of Faith and Trust in Jehovah

A lack of faith and trust in Jehovah can also lead to spiritual sickness. When believers face trials and challenges, they may begin to doubt God's goodness, love, and sovereignty, leading to a weakened faith and spiritual despair. Hebrews 11:6 reminds us, "And without faith, it is impossible to please him, for whoever would draw near to God must believe that he exists and that he rewards those who seek him." Cultivating a strong, unwavering faith is essential for spiritual health and resilience.

How to Recognize Symptoms of Spiritual Sickness

Recognizing the symptoms of spiritual sickness is the first step in addressing and overcoming it. These symptoms can manifest in various ways, including:

1. Emotional and Mental Distress

Spiritual sickness often manifests as emotional and mental distress, such as anxiety, depression, hopelessness, or overwhelming guilt. These emotions can be signals that something is amiss in one's spiritual life and that it needs to be addressed. Psalm 42:5 captures the psalmist's struggle with spiritual desolation: "Why are you cast down, O my soul, and why are you in turmoil within me? Hope in God; for I shall again praise him, my salvation."

2. Apathy and Indifference Toward Spiritual Matters

Apathy and indifference toward spiritual matters, such as a lack of interest in prayer, Bible study, or fellowship, can also be signs of spiritual sickness. When a believer no longer finds joy in spiritual practices or begins to neglect them altogether, it indicates a need for spiritual renewal. Revelation 3:15-16 warns the church in Laodicea about the dangers of spiritual lukewarmness: "I know your works: you are neither cold nor hot. Would that you were either cold or hot! So, because you are lukewarm, and neither hot nor cold, I will spit you out of my mouth."

3. Persistent Sin and Unrepentance

Persistent sin and a refusal to repent are clear indicators of spiritual sickness. When a believer continues in sinful behavior without seeking forgiveness or making efforts to change, it reflects a hardened heart and a need for spiritual intervention. Proverbs 28:13 warns, "Whoever conceals his transgressions will not prosper, but he who confesses and forsakes them will obtain mercy."

4. Disconnection from Jehovah and Others

A sense of disconnection from Jehovah and others, including feelings of isolation or alienation from the Christian community, can also be a symptom of spiritual sickness. This disconnection can lead to a deep sense of loneliness and despair, as described in Psalm 25:16-17: "Turn to me and be gracious to me, for I am lonely and afflicted. The troubles of my heart are enlarged; bring me out of my distresses."

Biblical Steps to Healing Spiritual Sickness

The Bible offers a comprehensive guide for healing from spiritual sickness, emphasizing the importance of repentance, restoration, and renewal. These steps are not merely theoretical but require practical, actionable efforts to restore spiritual health.

1. Confession and Repentance

The first and most crucial step in healing from spiritual sickness is confession and repentance. Confession involves acknowledging one's sins before Jehovah, without attempting to justify or minimize them. 1 John 1:9 assures us, "If we confess our sins, he is faithful and just to forgive us our sins and to cleanse us from all unrighteousness."

Repentance goes beyond confession, involving a genuine change of heart and behavior, turning away from sin and toward Jehovah.

David's prayer of repentance in Psalm 51 serves as a model for believers seeking healing from spiritual sickness. In verses 1-2, David pleads, "Have mercy on me, O God, according to your steadfast love; according to your abundant mercy blot out my transgressions. Wash me thoroughly from my iniquity, and cleanse me from my sin." David's heartfelt plea demonstrates the sincerity and humility required for true repentance.

2. Seeking Forgiveness and Reconciliation

After confessing and repenting of sin, it is essential to seek forgiveness and reconciliation, both with Jehovah and others. Forgiveness restores our relationship with God, while reconciliation mends broken relationships with others. Matthew 5:23-24 emphasizes the importance of reconciliation: "So if you are offering your gift at the altar and there remember that your brother has something against you, leave your gift there before the altar and go. First, be reconciled to your brother, and then come and offer your gift."

Forgiveness may also involve forgiving oneself, as holding onto guilt and shame can hinder spiritual healing. Isaiah 1:18 offers reassurance: "Come now, let us reason together, says Jehovah: though your sins are like scarlet, they shall be as white as snow; though they are red like crimson, they shall become like wool." This verse reminds believers that Jehovah's forgiveness is complete and that they should not continue to burden themselves with past sins once they have been forgiven.

3. Restoring Spiritual Disciplines

Restoring spiritual disciplines is vital for healing from spiritual sickness. Regular prayer, Bible study, worship, and fellowship provide the spiritual nourishment needed for growth and renewal. Acts 2:42 describes the early church's commitment to these disciplines: "And they devoted themselves to the apostles' teaching and the fellowship, to the breaking of bread and the prayers." This devotion to spiritual practices helped the early believers remain steadfast in their faith and connected to one another.

Developing a consistent prayer life is essential for maintaining spiritual health. Philippians 4:6 encourages believers to "not be anxious about anything, but in everything by prayer and supplication with thanksgiving let your requests be made known to God." Prayer not only brings peace but also strengthens our relationship with Jehovah, providing the guidance and strength needed to overcome spiritual sickness.

Bible study is another critical discipline for spiritual health. 2 Timothy 3:16-17 affirms the importance of Scripture in equipping believers for every good work: "All Scripture is breathed out by God and profitable for teaching, for reproof, for correction, and for training in righteousness, that the man of God may be complete, equipped for every good work." Regular study of God's Word deepens our understanding of His will and helps us apply His principles to our lives.

Fellowship with other believers is also essential for spiritual growth and accountability. Hebrews 10:24-25 urges believers to "consider how to stir up one another to love and good works, not neglecting to meet together, as is the habit of some, but encouraging one another, and all the more as you see the Day drawing near." Engaging in Christian community provides support, encouragement, and accountability, which are crucial for maintaining spiritual health.

4. Cultivating a Heart of Worship and Praise

Worship and praise are powerful tools for overcoming spiritual sickness. They shift our focus from our circumstances to Jehovah, reminding us of His greatness, love, and faithfulness. Psalm 100:4-5 encourages believers to "enter his gates with thanksgiving, and his courts with praise! Give thanks to him; bless his name! For Jehovah is good; his steadfast love endures forever, and his faithfulness to all generations."

Cultivating a heart of worship involves making worship a regular part of our daily lives, not just during church services. This can include singing hymns, offering prayers of thanksgiving, and reflecting on

God's attributes and works. Worship renews our spirit and strengthens our faith, helping us overcome the effects of spiritual sickness.

5. Trusting in Jehovah's Healing and Provision

Healing from spiritual sickness requires trusting in Jehovah's power and provision. Isaiah 53:5 speaks of the healing that comes through Jesus' sacrifice: "But he was wounded for our transgressions; he was crushed for our iniquities; upon him was the chastisement that brought us peace, and with his stripes, we are healed." This verse reminds believers that Jesus' suffering and death provide not only forgiveness of sins but also healing for our spiritual wounds.

Trusting in Jehovah's healing also involves relying on His timing and wisdom. Sometimes, the process of healing can be slow, and it may require patience and perseverance. James 5:16 encourages believers to pray for one another, acknowledging the power of prayer in bringing about healing: "Therefore, confess your sins to one another and pray for one another, that you may be healed. The prayer of a righteous person has great power as it is working."

6. Practicing Forgiveness and Reconciliation

Forgiveness and reconciliation are vital components of healing from spiritual sickness. Unforgiveness can lead to bitterness, which further deepens spiritual sickness. Colossians 3:13 instructs believers to "bear with one another and, if one has a complaint against another, forgiving each other; as the Lord has forgiven you, so you also must forgive." Forgiving others, as well as seeking forgiveness, restores relationships and clears the path for spiritual healing.

Reconciliation involves more than just forgiving; it requires actively working to restore broken relationships. Romans 12:18 advises, "If possible, so far as it depends on you, live peaceably with all." Taking steps to reconcile with others demonstrates humility and obedience to Jehovah's command to love one another.

7. Seeking Christian Counseling for Deeper Healing

In some cases, spiritual sickness may be deeply rooted in past trauma, unresolved emotional issues, or long-standing patterns of sin. In such instances, seeking the help of a Christian counselor can be beneficial. Proverbs 20:5 states, "The purpose in a man's heart is like deep water, but a man of understanding will draw it out." A skilled counselor can help you explore and address the underlying issues contributing to spiritual sickness.

Christian counseling integrates biblical principles with psychological insights, providing a holistic approach to healing. It offers a safe space to process emotions, confront past wounds, and develop strategies for overcoming spiritual challenges. Seeking counseling is not a sign of weakness but rather a proactive step toward spiritual wholeness.

8. Embracing God's Grace and Mercy

Finally, healing from spiritual sickness requires embracing God's grace and mercy. Ephesians 2:8-9 reminds us, "For by grace you have been saved through faith. And this is not your own doing; it is the gift of God, not a result of works, so that no one may boast." Understanding and accepting God's grace allows us to move forward in our spiritual journey, free from the burdens of guilt and shame.

Grace empowers us to live victoriously, even in the face of spiritual challenges. 2 Corinthians 12:9 encourages believers with these words: "But he said to me, 'My grace is sufficient for you, for my power is made perfect in weakness.' Therefore I will boast all the more gladly of my weaknesses, so that the power of Christ may rest upon me." Recognizing that God's grace is sufficient enables us to trust in His provision and continue striving for spiritual health.

The Role of Community in Overcoming Spiritual Sickness

While personal efforts are essential in overcoming spiritual sickness, the role of community should not be underestimated. The

Christian community provides support, encouragement, and accountability, which are crucial for maintaining spiritual health.

1. The Importance of Fellowship

Fellowship with other believers is a key component of spiritual health. It provides opportunities for mutual encouragement, learning, and growth. Acts 2:42 describes the early church's commitment to fellowship: "And they devoted themselves to the apostles' teaching and the fellowship, to the breaking of bread and the prayers." This commitment to community helped the early believers remain steadfast in their faith and supported one another in times of need.

Engaging in regular fellowship helps prevent spiritual isolation, which can exacerbate spiritual sickness. Whether through small groups, prayer meetings, or church services, staying connected to the body of Christ is vital for spiritual well-being.

2. Encouraging One Another

Encouragement is a powerful tool in overcoming spiritual sickness. Hebrews 10:24-25 urges believers to "consider how to stir up one another to love and good works, not neglecting to meet together, as is the habit of some, but encouraging one another, and all the more as you see the Day drawing near." Encouraging one another helps to lift spirits, strengthen faith, and renew hope.

Offering encouragement can take many forms, from a kind word or a thoughtful note to praying for someone or offering practical help. By encouraging one another, we fulfill the biblical mandate to "bear one another's burdens, and so fulfill the law of Christ" (Galatians 6:2).

3. Accountability and Discipleship

Accountability and discipleship are essential aspects of community life that help believers maintain spiritual health. Proverbs 27:17 states, "Iron sharpens iron, and one man sharpens another." Being accountable to others provides motivation to stay on the right path and avoid spiritual pitfalls.

Discipleship involves mentoring and being mentored, helping one another grow in faith and spiritual maturity. Matthew 28:19-20 commands believers to "go therefore and make disciples of all nations, baptizing them in the name of the Father and of the Son and of the Holy Spirit, teaching them to observe all that I have commanded you." Discipleship fosters spiritual growth and helps prevent spiritual sickness by providing guidance, support, and instruction.

Moving Forward: A Life of Spiritual Health and Wholeness

Overcoming spiritual sickness is not a one-time event but an ongoing process of growth, renewal, and transformation. By applying the biblical principles and practical strategies outlined in this chapter, believers can move forward in their spiritual journey, experiencing greater health, wholeness, and intimacy with Jehovah.

1. Continual Growth and Renewal

Spiritual health requires continual growth and renewal. 2 Peter 3:18 encourages believers to "grow in the grace and knowledge of our Lord and Savior Jesus Christ." This growth involves deepening our understanding of God's Word, developing spiritual disciplines, and allowing the Holy Spirit-inspired Word to transform our hearts and minds.

Continual growth also involves being open to correction and willing to change. Hebrews 12:11 reminds us, "For the moment all discipline seems painful rather than pleasant, but later it yields the peaceful fruit of righteousness to those who have been trained by it." Embracing God's discipline leads to spiritual maturity and health.

2. Embracing a Life of Service and Purpose

Living a life of service and purpose is essential for maintaining spiritual health. Ephesians 2:10 affirms, "For we are his workmanship, created in Christ Jesus for good works, which God prepared beforehand, that we should walk in them." Engaging in service to others and fulfilling our God-given purpose brings joy, fulfillment, and a sense of connection to the body of Christ.

Service can take many forms, from volunteering in the community to using our talents and gifts for the benefit of others. By serving others, we follow Jesus' example and contribute to the health and vitality of the Christian community.

3. Cultivating a Heart of Worship and Gratitude

Worship and gratitude are powerful tools for maintaining spiritual health. Psalm 100:4-5 encourages believers to "enter his gates with thanksgiving, and his courts with praise! Give thanks to him; bless his name! For Jehovah is good; his steadfast love endures forever, and his faithfulness to all generations." Cultivating a heart of worship and gratitude helps us stay focused on Jehovah's goodness and faithfulness, even in difficult times.

Regularly expressing gratitude for God's blessings, both big and small, helps to keep our hearts and minds centered on Him. Worship, whether through song, prayer, or reflection, draws us closer to Jehovah and strengthens our spiritual resilience.

4. Trusting in Jehovah's Promises

Finally, maintaining spiritual health requires trusting in Jehovah's promises. Romans 8:28 assures us, "And we know that for those who love God, all things work together for good, for those who are called according to his purpose." Trusting in God's promises gives us confidence and hope, even in the face of challenges and trials.

By holding onto Jehovah's promises, we can navigate the ups and downs of life with faith and perseverance, knowing that He is with us and will guide us through every situation.

CHAPTER 26 How Can Christians Overcome Temptation Through Biblical Counseling and Cognitive Behavioral Therapy?

Understanding the Nature of Temptation

Temptation is an inherent aspect of the human experience, deeply rooted in our fallen nature and the world we live in. From the earliest chapters of Genesis, we see how temptation played a critical role in humanity's fall. Satan, the adversary, used temptation to lure Adam and Eve into disobedience, which resulted in spiritual death and separation from Jehovah (Genesis 3:1-6). This historical event marks the beginning of the ongoing struggle between yielding to temptation and maintaining faithfulness to Jehovah.

Temptation is an enticement to sin, presenting itself in various forms—whether it be through lust, greed, pride, or other sinful desires. James 1:14-15 provides insight into how temptation operates: "But each person is tempted when he is lured and enticed by his own desire. Then desire, when it has conceived, gives birth to sin, and sin, when it is fully grown, brings forth death." This scripture highlights the progression from temptation to sin and ultimately to spiritual death, underscoring the importance of resisting temptation from the outset.

However, it's important to recognize that temptation itself is not sin. Even Jesus, who was without sin, was tempted by Satan in the wilderness (Matthew 4:1-11). Yet, He overcame each temptation by relying on God's Word, setting an example for believers to follow.

Understanding that temptation is a test of faith rather than a sin itself can help Christians approach it with the right mindset.

The Spiritual and Psychological Dimensions of Temptation

Temptation affects both the spiritual and psychological dimensions of our lives. Spiritually, it seeks to weaken our relationship with Jehovah by drawing us away from His will and leading us into disobedience. Psychologically, temptation can play on our thoughts, emotions, and desires, making it a complex challenge to overcome. Cognitive Behavioral Therapy (CBT) provides valuable tools for understanding and addressing the psychological aspects of temptation, while biblical counseling offers the spiritual guidance needed to resist and overcome it.

CBT teaches that our thoughts influence our emotions and behaviors, and by identifying and challenging negative or irrational thoughts, we can change our behavior. This approach aligns with the biblical principle found in Romans 12:2, which instructs believers to "be transformed by the renewal of your mind." By renewing our minds through Scripture and godly thinking, we can better resist the allure of temptation.

The Source of Temptation: Understanding the Adversary

The Bible identifies Satan as the primary source of temptation. Referred to as "the tempter" in Matthew 4:3, Satan's goal is to lead believers astray and cause them to fall into sin. Ephesians 6:11-12 warns, "Put on the whole armor of God, that you may be able to stand against the schemes of the devil. For we do not wrestle against flesh and blood, but against the rulers, against the authorities, against the cosmic powers over this present darkness, against the spiritual forces of evil in the heavenly places." This passage emphasizes the spiritual nature of our battle against temptation and the need for divine armor to withstand Satan's attacks.

However, not all temptation comes directly from Satan. The Bible also teaches that we are tempted by our own sinful nature. Jeremiah 17:9 states, "The heart is deceitful above all things, and desperately sick; who can understand it?" Our sinful nature inclines us toward evil, making us susceptible to temptation. Recognizing the dual sources of temptation—external (Satan) and internal (sinful desires)—is crucial in developing a comprehensive strategy to overcome it.

Why Is Temptation So Challenging?

Temptation is challenging because it appeals to our natural desires and weaknesses. Genesis 6:5 describes the pervasive wickedness of humanity before the flood: "Jehovah saw that the wickedness of man was great in the earth, and that every intention of the thoughts of his heart was only evil continually." Even after the flood, the nature of humanity remained inclined toward sin, as noted in Genesis 8:21, where Jehovah acknowledges that "the intention of man's heart is evil from his youth."

The Apostle Paul also struggled with temptation, as he explains in Romans 7:21-25: "So I find it to be a law that when I want to do right, evil lies close at hand. For I delight in the law of God, in my inner being, but I see in my members another law waging war against the law of my mind and making me captive to the law of sin that dwells in my members. Wretched man that I am! Who will deliver me from this body of death? Thanks be to God through Jesus Christ our Lord!" Paul's transparency about his internal battle with sin provides encouragement for believers who face similar struggles, reminding us that victory is found in Jesus Christ.

Temptation is also challenging because it often comes at times of weakness or vulnerability. Satan approached Jesus in the wilderness after He had fasted for forty days and was physically weak (Matthew 4:2). Similarly, Satan attacks believers when they are tired, discouraged, or facing trials. Recognizing these vulnerable moments can help us be more vigilant and prepared to resist temptation.

The Role of the Holy Spirit-Inspired Word in Overcoming Temptation

The Holy Spirit-inspired Word of God is our most powerful weapon against temptation. Ephesians 6:17 refers to the Word of God as "the sword of the Spirit," indicating its role in spiritual warfare. When Jesus was tempted in the wilderness, He responded to each of Satan's temptations with Scripture, saying, "It is written" (Matthew 4:4, 7, 10). This demonstrates the importance of knowing and applying Scripture to combat temptation.

Psalm 119:11 also highlights the protective power of God's Word: "I have stored up your word in my heart, that I might not sin against you." By internalizing Scripture, we can recall it in moments of temptation, allowing it to guide our thoughts and actions. Regular and meaningful Bible study helps us to understand God's will, discern right from wrong, and develop the spiritual maturity needed to resist temptation.

Prayer is another vital component in overcoming temptation. Jesus instructed His disciples to "watch and pray that you may not enter into temptation. The spirit indeed is willing, but the flesh is weak" (Matthew 26:41). Prayer connects us with Jehovah's strength, enabling us to stand firm against temptation. It is through prayer that we seek God's help, wisdom, and guidance in moments of weakness.

How to Cultivate Self-Control to Resist Temptation

Self-control is an essential quality for resisting temptation, as it enables us to manage our desires and impulses in alignment with God's will. Galatians 5:22-23 lists self-control as one of the fruits of the Spirit, indicating that it is a characteristic that should be evident in the life of every believer. However, cultivating self-control requires intentional effort and reliance on Jehovah's strength.

1. Pray for the Holy Spirit-Inspired Word to Penetrate the Heart

The first step in cultivating self-control is to pray for the Holy Spirit-inspired Word to penetrate our hearts. Hebrews 4:12 describes the Word of God as "living and active, sharper than any two-edged sword, piercing to the division of soul and of spirit, of joints and of marrow, and discerning the thoughts and intentions of the heart." When the Word of God takes root in our hearts, it transforms our desires, aligning them with Jehovah's will.

2. Act on Behalf of the Prayer

Prayer must be paired with action. James 2:17 reminds us that "faith by itself, if it does not have works, is dead." After praying for self-control, we must take practical steps to cultivate it. This includes identifying areas of weakness, avoiding situations that trigger temptation, and making a plan to resist it. Proverbs 4:26-27 advises, "Ponder the path of your feet; then all your ways will be sure. Do not swerve to the right or to the left; turn your foot away from evil." Planning and preparation are key components of self-control.

3. Feed on God's Word and Supportive Literature

Feeding on God's Word is essential for developing self-control. As mentioned earlier, regular and meaningful Bible study equips us with the knowledge and wisdom needed to resist temptation. In addition to Scripture, supportive literature that aligns with biblical principles can provide further insight and encouragement. Proverbs 2:6 declares, "For Jehovah gives wisdom; from his mouth come knowledge and understanding." Seeking wisdom from God's Word and godly literature strengthens our resolve to live according to His will.

4. Engage in Regular and Meaningful Bible Study

Bible study is not just about acquiring knowledge; it's about transforming our minds and hearts. Romans 12:2 encourages believers to "be transformed by the renewal of your mind." This transformation occurs as we meditate on Scripture, allowing it to shape our thoughts, attitudes, and actions. Engaging in regular and meaningful Bible study helps us to develop the self-control needed to resist temptation.

Responding to Failure: What to Do When We Fall into Temptation

Despite our best efforts, there may be times when we fail to exercise self-control and fall into temptation. When this happens, it is important to respond with humility, repentance, and renewed determination.

1. Approach Jehovah in Prayer

When we fall into temptation, our first response should be to approach Jehovah in prayer. Psalm 51:10 captures David's prayer for a clean heart after his sin with Bathsheba: "Create in me a clean heart, O God, and renew a right spirit within me." Jehovah is gracious and merciful, and He invites us to come to Him for forgiveness and restoration. Hebrews 4:16 encourages us to "draw near to the throne of grace, that we may receive mercy and find grace to help in time of need."

2. Seek Forgiveness and Restoration

1 John 1:9 assures us, "If we confess our sins, he is faithful and just to forgive us our sins and to cleanse us from all unrighteousness." Seeking forgiveness is a crucial step in restoring our relationship with Jehovah after falling into temptation. Psalm 32:5 reflects David's experience of confessing his sin and receiving forgiveness: "I acknowledged my sin to you, and I did not cover my iniquity; I said, 'I will confess my transgressions to Jehovah,' and you forgave the iniquity of my sin."

3. Resolve Not to Repeat the Same Mistake

After seeking forgiveness, it is important to resolve not to repeat the same mistake. This requires a renewed commitment to self-control and a proactive approach to avoiding temptation in the future. Philippians 3:13-14 encourages believers to "forget what lies behind and strain forward to what lies ahead, pressing on toward the goal for the prize of the upward call of God in Christ Jesus." By focusing on spiritual growth and maturity, we can overcome the setbacks of past failures.

The Importance of Community Support in Overcoming Temptation

Overcoming temptation is not something we have to do alone. The Christian community plays a vital role in supporting believers as they strive to resist temptation and grow in self-control.

1. The Role of Accountability Partners

Having an accountability partner can provide valuable support in overcoming temptation. Ecclesiastes 4:9-10 highlights the benefits of mutual support: "Two are better than one, because they have a good reward for their toil. For if they fall, one will lift up his fellow." An accountability partner can offer encouragement, prayer, and practical advice, helping us to stay on track in our spiritual journey.

2. The Value of Confession and Prayer

James 5:16 encourages believers to "confess your sins to one another and pray for one another, that you may be healed." Confession and prayer are powerful tools for overcoming temptation. When we confess our struggles to a trusted friend or mentor, we bring them into the light, where they can be addressed with God's help. Prayer, both personal and communal, invites Jehovah's strength and guidance into our lives, empowering us to resist temptation.

3. The Support of the Church Community

The church community provides a network of support for believers facing temptation. Hebrews 10:24-25 urges believers to "consider how to stir up one another to love and good works, not neglecting to meet together, as is the habit of some, but encouraging one another, and all the more as you see the Day drawing near." By staying connected to the body of Christ, we can receive the encouragement, teaching, and fellowship needed to stay strong in the face of temptation.

Developing a Long-Term Strategy for Overcoming Temptation

Overcoming temptation requires a long-term strategy that includes spiritual growth, accountability, and reliance on Jehovah's strength.

1. Commit to Lifelong Spiritual Growth

Spiritual growth is a lifelong journey that requires commitment and perseverance. 2 Peter 3:18 encourages believers to "grow in the grace and knowledge of our Lord and Savior Jesus Christ." By continually growing in our faith, we become better equipped to resist temptation and live in accordance with Jehovah's will.

2. Establish Regular Spiritual Disciplines

Regular spiritual disciplines, such as prayer, Bible study, fasting, and worship, help to strengthen our spiritual muscles and build resilience against temptation. 1 Timothy 4:7-8 advises believers to "train yourself for godliness; for while bodily training is of some value, godliness is of value in every way, as it holds promise for the present life and also for the life to come." Spiritual disciplines are essential for maintaining a strong and vibrant relationship with Jehovah.

3. Rely on Jehovah's Strength

Ultimately, our ability to overcome temptation depends on Jehovah's strength. Philippians 4:13 declares, "I can do all things through him who strengthens me." By relying on God's power rather than our own, we can face temptation with confidence, knowing that He is with us and will provide a way of escape (1 Corinthians 10:13).

4. Stay Vigilant and Prepared

1 Peter 5:8 warns believers to "be sober-minded; be watchful. Your adversary the devil prowls around like a roaring lion, seeking someone to devour." Staying vigilant and prepared helps us to anticipate and resist temptation before it takes hold. This includes being aware of our weaknesses, avoiding situations that could lead to sin, and being ready to respond with Scripture and prayer when temptation arises.

Conclusion: A Life of Victory Over Temptation

Overcoming temptation is a daily challenge, but with the guidance of Scripture, the support of the Christian community, and reliance on Jehovah's strength, it is possible to live a life of victory. By cultivating self-control, engaging in regular spiritual disciplines, and staying connected to the body of Christ, believers can resist temptation and grow in their faith, becoming more like Jesus Christ each day.

CHAPTER 27 How Can Christians Have the Mind of Christ and Be Biblically Minded?

Understanding the Mind of Christ

To fully grasp what it means to have the mind of Christ, we must first understand who Christ is and how He demonstrated His thinking. The Apostle Paul exhorts believers in Philippians 2:5, "Have this mind among yourselves, which is yours in Christ Jesus." This verse sets the foundation for understanding that having the mind of Christ is not just a suggestion but a command for those who follow Him. The mind of Christ is characterized by humility, obedience to God, and a self-sacrificial love for others. Jesus, although He was in the form of God, "did not count equality with God a thing to be grasped, but emptied himself, by taking the form of a servant, being born in the likeness of men" (Philippians 2:6-7). His life was marked by complete submission to the Father's will, even to the point of death on the cross (Philippians 2:8).

The mind of Christ also reflects perfect harmony with the Word of God. Jesus consistently quoted and lived by Scripture, showing that His thoughts were deeply rooted in the truth of God's Word. In Matthew 4:4, when Satan tempted Him, Jesus responded, "It is written, 'Man shall not live by bread alone, but by every word that comes from the mouth of God.'" This response highlights that the mind of Christ is one that depends entirely on the Scriptures for guidance, sustenance, and wisdom.

Therefore, to have the mind of Christ means to think, act, and live according to the principles laid out in the Bible, seeking to embody the humility, obedience, and love that Christ Himself demonstrated.

The Necessity of a Biblically Minded Life

Being biblically minded is essential for every Christian because it shapes our worldview, influences our decisions, and molds our character. The Bible is not just a collection of ancient texts; it is the living Word of God, "sharper than any two-edged sword, piercing to the division of soul and of spirit, of joints and of marrow, and discerning the thoughts and intentions of the heart" (Hebrews 4:12). A biblically minded person allows the Word of God to permeate every aspect of their life, guiding their thoughts, attitudes, and actions.

The Apostle Paul emphasizes the importance of a transformed mind in Romans 12:2, where he writes, "Do not be conformed to this world, but be transformed by the renewal of your mind, that by testing you may discern what is the will of God, what is good and acceptable and perfect." This transformation begins with immersing oneself in Scripture, allowing it to renew our minds and align our thoughts with God's will. Without a biblically minded approach, Christians are at risk of conforming to the patterns of this world, which are often contrary to God's standards.

Moreover, being biblically minded equips believers to resist the temptations and deceptions of the world. Psalm 119:11 states, "I have stored up your word in my heart, that I might not sin against you." When the Word of God is deeply ingrained in our hearts and minds, it acts as a safeguard against sin, helping us to live in a manner that honors Jehovah.

Why Is It a Challenge to Develop the Mind of Christ?

Developing the mind of Christ is a challenge because it requires a continuous and conscious effort to align our thoughts with Scripture, which often conflicts with our natural inclinations and the influences of the world. Genesis 6:5 reveals the inherent wickedness of human nature: "Jehovah saw that the wickedness of man was great in the earth, and that every intention of the thoughts of his heart was only evil continually." This tendency toward sin is further echoed in

Genesis 8:21, where Jehovah acknowledges that "the intention of man's heart is evil from his youth." These verses highlight the deep-rooted sinful nature that exists within every person, making it difficult to naturally think and act in a way that reflects the mind of Christ.

Jeremiah 17:9 adds to this understanding by declaring, "The heart is deceitful above all things, and desperately sick; who can understand it?" This scripture underscores the internal battle that believers face in striving to have the mind of Christ. Our hearts are prone to self-deception, leading us away from God's truth and toward sinful desires. The Apostle Paul also reflects on this struggle in Romans 7:21-25, where he describes the conflict between his desire to do good and the sinful nature within him. He writes, "So I find it to be a law that when I want to do right, evil lies close at hand. For I delight in the law of God, in my inner being, but I see in my members another law waging war against the law of my mind and making me captive to the law of sin that dwells in my members."

This ongoing struggle between the flesh and the spirit makes it challenging for believers to develop the mind of Christ. However, the very fact that Paul acknowledges this struggle and his ultimate victory through Jesus Christ gives hope to all Christians that it is possible to overcome these challenges by relying on the power of God's Word and the guidance of the Holy Spirit-inspired Scriptures.

How to Cultivate the Mind of Christ

Cultivating the mind of Christ is a process that requires dedication, prayer, and practical steps rooted in Scripture. Here's how Christians can actively work toward developing a mind that reflects Christ.

1. Pray for the Holy Spirit-Inspired Word to Transform Your Heart

The first and most crucial step in cultivating the mind of Christ is prayer. Believers must continually seek Jehovah's help in allowing His Word to penetrate and transform their hearts. As the Psalmist prays in Psalm 119:18, "Open my eyes, that I may behold wondrous things out of your law." This prayer acknowledges the need for divine illumination to understand and apply Scripture effectively. When the Word of God is deeply rooted in our hearts, it begins to shape our thoughts, desires, and actions in a way that aligns with the mind of Christ.

2. Act on Behalf of Your Prayer

Prayer must be accompanied by action. James 1:22 exhorts believers, "But be doers of the word, and not hearers only, deceiving yourselves." It's not enough to simply pray for transformation; we must also take practical steps to live out the truths we discover in Scripture. This includes studying the Bible regularly, meditating on its teachings, and applying its principles in our daily lives. By actively living out the Word, we cultivate a mindset that mirrors Christ's.

3. Engage in Regular and Meaningful Bible Study

Regular Bible study is essential for developing a biblically minded life. Psalm 1:2-3 describes the blessed man as one whose "delight is in the law of Jehovah, and on his law, he meditates day and night. He is like a tree planted by streams of water that yields its fruit in its season, and its leaf does not wither. In all that he does, he prospers." Meditating on Scripture day and night allows it to take root in our hearts, providing spiritual nourishment and stability. Engaging in meaningful Bible study helps us to internalize God's Word, enabling us to think and act according to His will.

4. Seek the Help of Godly Literature and Counsel

In addition to Scripture, godly literature and counsel can provide valuable insight and encouragement in developing the mind of Christ. Proverbs 15:22 states, "Without counsel plans fail, but with many advisers, they succeed." Seeking wisdom from trusted Christian mentors, books, and resources can help us to gain a deeper understanding of Scripture and apply it effectively in our lives. This, in turn, helps to shape our thinking and align it with the mind of Christ.

The Role of Self-Control in Cultivating the Mind of Christ

Self-control is a critical aspect of developing the mind of Christ. Galatians 5:22-23 lists self-control as one of the fruits of the Spirit, indicating that it is a quality that should be evident in the life of every believer. However, self-control is not something that comes naturally; it must be cultivated through intentional effort and reliance on Jehovah's strength.

1. Recognize the Importance of Self-Control

Self-control is essential for resisting temptation and living in a manner that honors Jehovah. Proverbs 25:28 warns, "A man without self-control is like a city broken into and left without walls." Without self-control, we are vulnerable to the attacks of the enemy and the desires of the flesh. Cultivating self-control helps us to manage our thoughts, emotions, and actions in a way that reflects the mind of Christ.

2. Understand the Challenge of Self-Control

As mentioned earlier, developing self-control is challenging because it requires us to resist our natural inclinations and the influences of the world. Genesis 6:5 and Jeremiah 17:9 remind us of the inherent wickedness of the human heart, making it difficult to exercise self-control. However, the very fact that Scripture acknowledges this struggle should encourage believers to seek Jehovah's help in cultivating this essential quality.

3. Practical Steps to Cultivate Self-Control

Practical steps to cultivate self-control include setting boundaries, avoiding situations that trigger sinful desires, and seeking accountability from fellow believers. Proverbs 4:23 advises, "Keep your heart with all vigilance, for from it flow the springs of life." By guarding our hearts and minds, we can better resist the temptations that seek to pull us away from Jehovah's will.

Responding to Failures: How to Rebuild and Strengthen the Mind of Christ

There will be times when we fail to exercise self-control or fall short of having the mind of Christ. When this happens, it is important to respond in a way that leads to restoration and spiritual growth.

1. Approach Jehovah in Prayer

When we fail, the first step should be to approach Jehovah in prayer, seeking His forgiveness and strength to overcome future temptations. Psalm 51:9-11 records David's prayer for forgiveness after his sin with Bathsheba: "Hide your face from my sins, and blot out all my iniquities. Create in me a clean heart, O God, and renew a right spirit within me." David's example shows the importance of repentance and seeking Jehovah's help in times of failure.

2. Seek Forgiveness and Restoration

1 John 1:9 assures believers that "if we confess our sins, he is faithful and just to forgive us our sins and to cleanse us from all unrighteousness." Confessing our sins to Jehovah and seeking His forgiveness is crucial for restoring our relationship with Him. Psalm 32:5 reflects David's experience of confessing his sin and receiving forgiveness: "I acknowledged my sin to you, and I did not cover my iniquity; I said, 'I will confess my transgressions to Jehovah,' and you forgave the iniquity of my sin."

3. Resolve Not to Repeat the Same Mistake

After seeking forgiveness, it is important to resolve not to repeat the same mistake. Philippians 3:13-14 encourages believers to "forget what lies behind and strain forward to what lies ahead, pressing on toward the goal for the prize of the upward call of God in Christ Jesus." This requires a renewed commitment to self-control and a proactive approach to avoiding temptation in the future.

Encouraging One Another to Develop the Mind of Christ

Developing the mind of Christ is not something we do in isolation; it requires the support and encouragement of the Christian community.

1. The Role of Accountability Partners

Having an accountability partner can provide valuable support in developing the mind of Christ. Ecclesiastes 4:9-10 highlights the benefits of mutual support: "Two are better than one because they have a good reward for their toil. For if they fall, one will lift up his fellow." An accountability partner can offer encouragement, prayer, and practical advice, helping us to stay on track in our spiritual journey.

2. The Value of Confession and Prayer

James 5:16 encourages believers to "confess your sins to one another and pray for one another, that you may be healed." Confession and prayer are powerful tools for spiritual growth. When we confess our struggles to a trusted friend or mentor, we bring them into the light, where they can be addressed with Jehovah's help. Prayer, both personal and communal, invites God's strength and guidance into our lives, empowering us to develop the mind of Christ.

3. The Support of the Church Community

The church community provides a network of support for believers striving to have the mind of Christ. Hebrews 10:24-25 urges believers to "consider how to stir up one another to love and good works, not neglecting to meet together, as is the habit of some, but encouraging one another, and all the more as you see the Day drawing near." By staying connected to the body of Christ, we can receive the encouragement, teaching, and fellowship needed to grow in our faith and develop a mindset that reflects Christ.

Conclusion: A Lifelong Journey Toward the Mind of Christ

Developing the mind of Christ is a lifelong journey that requires dedication, prayer, and practical steps rooted in Scripture. By immersing ourselves in God's Word, cultivating self-control, and seeking the support of the Christian community, we can grow in our faith and become more like Christ each day. It is a journey marked by progress and setbacks, but with the guidance of the Holy Spirit-inspired Scriptures and the encouragement of fellow believers, it is a journey that leads to spiritual maturity and a deeper relationship with Jehovah.

CHAPTER 28 Draw Comfort in That We Worship a God Who Is Ready to Forgive

A God Who Is Ready to Forgive

The Bible clearly reveals that Jehovah is a God who is ready to forgive. His willingness to extend mercy and forgiveness is a central theme throughout Scripture, demonstrating His profound love and understanding of the human condition. In Psalm 86:5, it is written, "For you, O Jehovah, are good and forgiving, abounding in steadfast love to all who call upon you." This verse encapsulates the nature of Jehovah as a God who is not only good but also eager to forgive those who turn to Him.

The depth of this forgiveness is further illustrated in Psalm 38:4, 8, where the Psalmist expresses the weight of his sin and his overwhelming need for God's mercy: "For my iniquities have gone over my head; like a heavy burden, they are too heavy for me… I am feeble and crushed; I groan because of the tumult of my heart." These verses convey the burden of sin that humanity carries, but they also point to the relief that comes from knowing that Jehovah is ready to lift that burden through forgiveness.

In the New Testament, Paul emphasizes the importance of forgiving others as God forgives us in 2 Corinthians 2:5-11. He urges the church to forgive and comfort the one who has caused grief, warning them against allowing Satan to take advantage of their lack of forgiveness. This passage underscores the principle that as recipients of Jehovah's forgiveness, we are also called to extend that same forgiveness to others, reflecting His character in our own lives.

Proverbs 28:13 also speaks to the readiness of Jehovah to forgive those who confess and forsake their sins: "Whoever conceals his transgressions will not prosper, but he who confesses and forsakes them will obtain mercy." This verse highlights the importance of repentance and the assurance of forgiveness when we turn away from sin and seek God's mercy.

Why God Is Ready to Forgive

Understanding why Jehovah is ready to forgive involves recognizing His deep knowledge of our human frailty and His unwavering love for us. Psalm 103:14 reminds us, "For he knows our frame; he remembers that we are dust." Jehovah's understanding of our weaknesses does not lead to condemnation but rather to a readiness to forgive. He is fully aware of the struggles and temptations we face, and His forgiveness is an expression of His compassion for our plight.

Jeremiah 18:2-6 provides a powerful illustration of Jehovah's sovereignty and mercy through the imagery of a potter and clay. The passage describes how Jehovah, like a potter, can reshape and reform us despite our imperfections. This metaphor underscores the idea that Jehovah is not quick to discard or destroy us when we falter but is instead willing to forgive and mold us into vessels of honor.

Romans 3:9 and Romans 5:21 further explain that all have sinned and fallen short of the glory of God, yet through Jesus Christ, grace reigns through righteousness leading to eternal life. The apostle Paul acknowledges the pervasive nature of sin but also emphasizes the superabundance of grace available through Christ. This grace is the foundation of Jehovah's readiness to forgive; it is not based on our merit but on His love and the redemptive work of His Son.

Paul's struggle with sin, as described in Romans 7:17, 20, 23, 25, 21, 24, echoes the universal human experience of battling against sinful desires. Yet, even in this struggle, there is hope because of Jehovah's readiness to forgive. Psalm 51:17 highlights the importance of a contrite heart in receiving God's forgiveness: "The sacrifices of God are a broken spirit; a broken and contrite heart, O God, you will not despise." Jehovah's willingness to forgive is not contingent on our ability to live perfectly but on our humility and repentance.

How Completely Does God Forgive?

Jehovah's forgiveness is not partial or conditional; it is complete and total. When He forgives, He removes our sins as far as the east is from the west, as Psalm 103:12 poetically describes: "As far as the east is from the west, so far does he remove our transgressions from us." This verse captures the infinite extent of God's forgiveness, emphasizing that once forgiven, our sins are no longer held against us.

In Psalm 32:5, David testifies to the freedom that comes from confessing sin and receiving Jehovah's forgiveness: "I acknowledged my sin to you, and I did not cover my iniquity; I said, 'I will confess my transgressions to Jehovah,' and you forgave the iniquity of my sin." This verse highlights the transformative power of forgiveness, which lifts the burden of guilt and restores the sinner to a right relationship with God.

The completeness of Jehovah's forgiveness is further illustrated in Isaiah 1:18, where He invites sinners to reason with Him: "Though your sins are like scarlet, they shall be as white as snow; though they are red like crimson, they shall become like wool." This verse underscores the radical change that occurs when Jehovah forgives—sins that once stained are completely cleansed, leaving the sinner pure and renewed.

Isaiah 38:17 provides another powerful image of forgiveness: "Behold, it was for my welfare that I had great bitterness; but in love, you have delivered my life from the pit of destruction, for you have cast all my sins behind your back." The imagery of casting sins behind God's back conveys the idea that He no longer sees or remembers them once they are forgiven.

Micah 7:18-19 also speaks to the depth of Jehovah's forgiveness: "Who is a God like you, pardoning iniquity and passing over transgression for the remnant of his inheritance? He does not retain his anger forever because he delights in steadfast love. He will again have compassion on us; he will tread our iniquities underfoot. You will cast all our sins into the depths of the sea." This passage portrays Jehovah as a compassionate and loving God who not only forgives but also completely eradicates the memory of our sins.

In the New Testament, Jesus teaches His disciples to pray for forgiveness in the Lord's Prayer, saying, "And forgive us our debts, as we also have forgiven our debtors" (Matthew 6:12) and "And forgive us our sins, for we ourselves forgive everyone who is indebted to us" (Luke 11:4). These verses affirm that Jehovah's forgiveness is not only complete but also a model for how we should forgive others.

Acts 3:19 reinforces the idea that forgiveness brings times of refreshing: "Repent therefore, and turn back, that your sins may be blotted out, that times of refreshing may come from the presence of the Lord." When Jehovah forgives, He blots out our sins, removing them entirely from our record and restoring our fellowship with Him.

God Will Remember Their Sin No More

One of the most comforting promises in Scripture is that Jehovah, once He forgives, remembers our sins no more. Jeremiah 31:34 declares, "And no longer shall each one teach his neighbor and each his brother, saying, 'Know Jehovah,' for they shall all know me, from the least of them to the greatest, declares Jehovah. For I will forgive their iniquity, and I will remember their sin no more." This verse assures us that Jehovah's forgiveness is so complete that He chooses to forget our sins, never bringing them up again.

The story of David's sin with Bathsheba and his subsequent repentance in 2 Samuel 11:1-17 and 12:13 illustrates this principle. Although David's sin was grave, Jehovah forgave him when he genuinely repented, and while there were consequences for his actions, Jehovah did not hold the sin against David forever. This narrative demonstrates that while sin has consequences, Jehovah's forgiveness is final, and He does not keep a record of our wrongs once we have repented.

Romans 15:4 reminds us that "whatever was written in former days was written for our instruction, that through endurance and the encouragement of the Scriptures we might have hope." The stories of forgiveness in the Bible serve as a source of encouragement for believers today, reminding us that Jehovah's readiness to forgive is as relevant now as it was in the days of the patriarchs and prophets.

What About the Consequences?

While Jehovah's forgiveness is complete, it does not always remove the consequences of our actions. Galatians 6:7 warns, "Do not be deceived: God is not mocked, for whatever one sows, that will he also reap." This verse highlights the principle of sowing and reaping, which means that our actions have consequences, even when we are forgiven.

James 1:13 emphasizes that God does not tempt anyone, but we are tempted by our own desires. When we give in to these desires and sin, there are natural consequences that follow. These consequences are not a sign that Jehovah has not forgiven us, but rather a result of the choices we have made.

The story of David, as mentioned earlier, is a poignant example of this truth. In 2 Samuel 12:9-12, after David's sin with Bathsheba, the prophet Nathan confronts him, and while David is forgiven, Jehovah declares that there will be consequences for his actions. David's household would suffer turmoil, and the child born from his sin would die. This narrative illustrates that forgiveness does not always negate the consequences of our sins, but it does restore our relationship with Jehovah.

Leviticus chapter 6 outlines the guilt offerings required for various sins under the Mosaic Law, demonstrating that while forgiveness was available, restitution or other actions were often required as a consequence of the sin. This principle carries over into the New Covenant, where forgiveness through Christ is freely given, but we may still need to make amends or face the consequences of our actions.

Colossians 2:13-14 speaks to the completeness of Jehovah's forgiveness through Christ: "And you, who were dead in your trespasses… God made alive together with him, having forgiven us all our trespasses, by canceling the record of debt that stood against us with its legal demands. This he set aside, nailing it to the cross." This passage emphasizes that while our sins are forgiven, and the debt is canceled, we may still experience the earthly consequences of those sins.

Jesus teaches in Matthew 5:23-24 that reconciliation with others is necessary when seeking Jehovah's forgiveness. If we have wronged someone, we are to make amends before offering our gift at the altar. This teaches us that while Jehovah forgives, we have a responsibility to address the impact of our sins on others.

Hebrews 10:21-22 encourages us to draw near to Jehovah with a sincere heart in full assurance of faith, having our hearts sprinkled clean from an evil conscience and our bodies washed with pure water. This passage reminds us that even when we face the consequences of our actions, we can approach Jehovah with confidence, knowing that His forgiveness is complete.

Proverbs 3:11-12 and Hebrews 12:5-11 teach that Jehovah disciplines those He loves, and this discipline, while sometimes painful, is for our good. It is a sign of His love and a means of helping us grow in righteousness. The consequences of our actions can be a form of this loving discipline, guiding us to make better choices in the future.

Finally, 1 John 1:9 assures us that "if we confess our sins, he is faithful and just to forgive us our sins and to cleanse us from all unrighteousness." This verse reinforces the idea that Jehovah's forgiveness is available to all who seek it, and while we may face the consequences of our sins, His forgiveness is always complete and final.

www.ingramcontent.com/pod-product-compliance
Lightning Source LLC
Chambersburg PA
CBHW031130090426
42738CB00008B/1037

* 9 7 8 1 9 4 5 7 5 7 2 2 8 *